WRITING WILLIAM

BY

Thomas Alexander

Writing William by Thomas Alexander

Direct Light Publishing
45 Dudley Court, Endell Street, London, WC2H 9RF

Permissions may be sought directly from NY Publishing Rights Department
45 Dudley Court, Endell Street, London, WC2H 9RF
Library of Congress Cataloguing in Publication Data
Application submitted.
British Library Cataloguing in Publication Data
Application submitted.
04 05 06 07 08 10 9 8 7 6 5 4 3 2

–

Cover design by SimplyA

DIRECT

LIGHT

WRITING WILLIAM
A Play by Thomas Alexander
A Comedy in IV Acts.
Synopsis

A comedy set over four acts, Writing William follows a young, aspiring playwright who, in order to get his work on stage, forges a Shakespeare play.

Basing the play on the relationship between Henry II and Eleanor of Aquitaine during the murder of Thomas Becket, the playwright, Will, starts to see it mirror his own failing marriage as he struggles to find approval from an unforgiving spouse. Backed by a working class billionaire and supported by an array of aging actors, the lead of which is mute, Will finds cathartic release in the writing of the play and it's impending production, but he hasn't taken into account just how gullible the theatre going public truly are. With the play a hit, he is faced with the choice of coming clean and reaping the rewards at the risk of being shunned by his audience, or staying true to his art.

A comedic farce, Writing William blends Shakespearian dialogue with modern humor and innovative staging to look at the relationship of the artist and his art, the burden of success upon a relationship and the true cost of producing a play.

Number of Characters:	8-10
Setting:	New York Bar / Theatre

ABOUT THE AUTHOR

Thomas Alexander has worked in almost all forms of theatre, from opera to children's performances, working as everything from stage hand to costume designer, and has seen his work translated into four different languages and performed as far afield as America and Afghanistan.

His plays; *Writing William, Begat, Great & Murder Me Gently* along with his novel; *A Scattering Of Orphans* have been published by DIRECT LIGHT.

Also by the Author

PLAYS

Happiness
Murder Me Gently
The Family
Begat
The Crossroads Country
Great
The Visitor
When Dusk Brings Glory
The Recruitment Officer
Writer's Block
The Last Christmas
Writing William
The Big Match

ONE ACT PLAYS

Four Widows and A Funeral
For Arts Sake
The TV
Life TM
The Dance

ADAPTATIONS

William Shakespeare's' R3
Othello

NOVELS

A Scattering Of Orphans

FOREWORD

There are very few things in life more satisfying than producing your first play, especially when it gives you licence to write faux Shakespearian verse.

Shakespeare is, to anyone in the world of theatre, a god, one who we measure ourselves up to and fail to do justice by. There are, after all, more books written about Shakespeare than anyone else in history, except presumably John Lennon. As one of the characters in the play cribs, *'We all lie in the gutter and stare up at his stars.'* If you're an actor, there is no finer accolade than being well-reviewed in a Shakespeare play. If you're a director, finding the perfect format for the play is career deciding, and if you're a producer… Well, having a successful Shakespeare play run in your theatre is akin to having a licence to print money.

For writers, though, there is no such divine succession. Yes, you can edit one of his greats, to try to find something new for it to say, but really – who cares about editors?! (I'm joking!) Writers are like ships without a compass. We set sail in a direction, hoping to find land, never taking note of signs that proclaim 'here be dragons' and 'the edge of the world this way.' Shakespeare has survived over 400 years of near constant performance, but we're just trying to get through opening night. The character who argues against our hero's plan to write a fake Shakespearean play was no doubt a sizable part of my own conscience begging me not to commit career suicide with my first production when he insisted that:

Shakespeare is! One cannot simply create Antony, or Cleopatra. They are Platonic forms! Existing since time immortal within the consciousness of man and expressed, nay imparted, to us by the bard! We are all under his shadow, it is true. We all find our skies dotted with his cloud. But write Shakespeare? A man could no more breathe words than he could again Ophelia! Or Brutus. Katharina!

Luckily, strong willpower and tremendous amounts of alcohol showed him who's boss.

I won't go into the boring details of how the play went up or the process involved – though if you are interested there are more details in the original playbill at the back of this publication – but I will say this: This is a work of youth. It takes a young man to have the audacity to attempt something this blatant. As we grow older in our art we become more careful, more circumspect. We shy away from projects that will cause consternation, or which will divide, unless of course division is our intention.

I've written far more politically divisive plays than this, and I might have even have attempted more audacious comedies. But I do wonder if I would leave myself, at this point in my writing, this open to the level of derision that could only come from writing faux Shakespeare, and that's sad.

C.S. Lewis believed that we read to know we're not alone, and if indeed that is true perhaps an artist creates in the hope they're not. I see the world this way, artists everywhere cry! Is anyone with me? For the comic, whether writer or stand-up, this rings even more true. Will anyone laugh along with us? Is this even funny? These are questions only ever answered by the silence of the stalls.

I purposefully stayed away from iambic pentameter in this piece of writing. It would have sounded falser than false, and the seamless slips sliding between reality and fiction in Act Two wouldn't have worked nearly as well.

If, therefore, you look too closely at the imitated Shakespearian dialogue in Writing William, you will find much to deride. But if you look at it as a young playwright, writing for a young theatre audience, hopefully I won't be alone. Hopefully it will make you laugh.

Four hundred and fifty or so years ago, a young playwrite did much the same. Bending the statutes of the day he borrowed and built on the best around him to become the worlds most famous writer and will no doubt go on to the be the longest lived as well.

I sincerely doubt I'll be around half that long but at least I can say I paid homage.

Thomas Alexander – 2014

Cast of Characters

No of cast: 8-10

WILL (William Burrows) Playwright. In his late twenties, early thirties,

SARAH (Sarah Burrows) His wife. Twenties.

KEVIN An English actor. Fifties.

ERIC Barman, actor and stagehand. Forties / Fifties.

TIM An actor. Mute. Mid thirties.

BOB (Robert) Billionaire industrialist & financier. Fifties.

SAM (Samantha) His wife / Actress. Late twenties. Aging Model.

JIM LOVITZ Movie producer. A well-educated, well-read, well-dressed charmer.

FOOL A Shakespearean Character.

ANNOUNCER Off stage.

NOTE; In the original Tokyo based production of the play the part of Fool was doubled with the character of Eric. This particular combination worked well and directors would be well advised to consider it as an option.

WRITING WILLIAM

Writing William was originally performed in Tokyo at 'What the Dickens' in Ebisu in 2006

Produced by New Worlds Theatre it was directed by Alec Harris.

The part of the Fool was coupled with the character of Eric, the barman.

Will	Chris Parham
Sarah	Naoko Sheena
Kevin	Martin Burns
Eric/Fool	Antun Percec
Tim	Laz Breezer
Bob	Patrick Smith
Sam	Christine Bishard
Jim Lovitz	Bob Werely

The play contained an extra Act with two extra characters.

Teddy	Rebecca Romans
Nathan	Mike Mitchell

WRITING WILLIAM

ACT 1

Scene I – The Trap Door

WITH THE CURTAIN STILL DOWN WE HEAR THE UNHEARD CONVERSATIONS OF A CROWDED BAR. BEER GLASSES CHINK, WOMEN LAUGH, AND MEN TALK LOUDLY SO AS TO BE HEARD. EVERY-ONE SEEMS TO BE ENJOYING THEMSELVES.

ANNOUNCER   Ladies and Gentlemen! Two minutes to curtain. Please take your seats for the second act. Thank you.

THE CROWD SLOWLY DISSIPATES. WE HEAR THE HEAVINESS OF FOOTSTEPS ON STAIRS AS THE CROWD LEAVES THE BAR. THE TALK FADES AWAY AS THEY GO.

CURTAINS.

WE OPEN ON AN ENGLISH PUB, LOCATED IN A BASEMENT BENEATH AN OFF-BROADWAY THEA-TRE IN NEW YORK.

LINED WITH OAK BEAMS AND A CHERRY WOOD BAR, THE ROOM IS THE EPITOME OF A THEA-TRE PUB, WITH PICTURES OF ACTORS PAST AND PRESENT ADORNING THE WALLS AROUND THE BAR, INCLUDING, NEAR THE BAR, A SIGNED PHO-TOGRAPH OF DYLAN THOMAS.

STAGE LEFT A FLIGHT OF STAIRS RUNS UP TO A DOOR ON THE SECOND LEVEL, AND IS THE MAIN

ENTRANCE TO THE BAR. STAGE RIGHT ARE TWO
DOORS TO THE RESTROOMS, MALE AND FEMALE
RESPECTIVELY.

CENTRE STAGE AT THE BAR SIT THREE MEN:
WILL, TIM AND KEVIN, THE LATTER TWO REG-
ULARS, TIM OFF AND AWAY FROM THEM, KEVIN
CLOSER TO WILL.

BEHIND THE BAR STANDS ERIC, THE BARMAN,
CLEANING UP THE DREGS FROM WHAT HAS
OBVIOUSLY BEEN A RELATIVELY LARGE CROWD
UNTIL RECENTLY.

AT THE TOP OF THE STAIRS, THE FOOL, DRESSED
IN SHAKESPEAREAN COSTUME, IS HOLDING EMP-
TY PINT GLASSES, SHOOING THE LAST OF THE
CUSTOMERS OUT OF THE BAR.

FOOL Come. Go! Up these stairs and out I say.

Why drinkest thou when there's a play!

Catch you now the second act,

A joy, I swear, or money back!

For everyone loves plays a' clever

(SOTTO) Written not by Sir Lloyd Webber.

THE FOOL TURNS AND HEADS BACK OVER TO
THE BAR, ADDRESSING THE AUDIENCE.

FOOL Why stay you, now? There's naught to see

(HE GESTURES TO THE BAR)

But God's sweet human mockery.

You stay? Well then. I guess all is well,

But here there's just one tale to tell.

Four they are, but all are one:

(POINTING TO TIM) A fault.

(TO ERIC) A fool.

(TO KEVIN) A drunken bum.

(HE STOPS AT WILL)

And here, a man who sits in words,

His bowels twisted up in curls.
For he hath learnt of all man's fate;
The wife you love, will surely hate.
A failure he, for up above
The audience shows his play no love.
(ASIDE) And why should they, for it's clear to see
There's no rhythm, cadence, or poetry.
(ALOUD) So sits he now, and drinks the last
Of all he has, his petty cash.
Waiting for his goodly wife,
To nurture him, with hook and knife.
(HE COMES TO THE EDGE OF THE STAGE)
Still stay you? Thought I am the fool.
I tolerate no view, by rule!
But come, you're here, what's let is let.
They'll speak, but not in coup-a-let.
EXIT FOOL STAGE LEFT.
ERIC   (TO WILL) Not going up then?
WILL   (NOT LOOKING UP) No.
ERIC   Not your thing, eh?
WILL   (FORLORN) So it would seem.
ERIC   Shame though. I mean, second act might be better. You never know.
WILL   Right.
ERIC   Hard to tell with a new performance. (WILL DOESN'T RESPOND) Modern, is it?
WILL   Something like that.
ERIC   These new lads. They try their best you know, but in the end… Wonder what it's about?
WILL   (LOOKING UP) It's a satire on mankind's continued inability to see themselves as more than a single unconnected consciousness. It's a humorous glance at the loss of social connection in an increasingly selfish world. It's two hours and forty-five minutes of unending banter,

mixing social class and racial profiling in an attempt to underpin the very existence of the human soul, if you must know.

ERIC   Ah, well. Maybe it'll get better in the second act. Want another one?

WILL HANDS HIM THE GLASS SULLENLY AND ERIC TURNS TO FILL IT UP.

FROM HIS PLACE AT THE BAR, KEVIN RAISES HIS GLASS AND COUGHS. WILL TRIES TO IGNORE HIM BUT KEVIN COUGHS LOUDER THIS TIME AND WILL IS FORCED TO RECOGNISE HIM.

KEVIN   (RAISING HIS GLASS) If one is pouring?

WILL LOOKS AT ERIC, WHO LOOKS AT HIM APPREHENSIVELY, HIS HAND POISED OVER A SECOND GLASS, WILLING HIM TO BUY KEVIN A DRINK.

WILL   (WITH A SHRUG) Suit yourself.

ERIC BEGINS TO POUR.

KEVIN   You sir, are a gent. (WILL WAVES IT OFF) No, I will not have it otherwise! (KEVIN CHANGES SEATS TO BE NEARER TO WILL WHO CLEARLY DOES NOT WANT HIM TO, AND ERIC DELIVERS THE TWO DRINKS BEFORE THEM) You are a gent and a scholar if you have chosen the bottle before (HE POINTS TO THE ROOF) the bard for, as Dylan Thomas himself once said to me, 'Fuck all words for a pint of whisky and a quick shag.' Though I hasten to add those are not my words but his own.

WILL   I see.

KEVIN   (PONTIFICATING) 'Twas the night he died…

WILL   I thought he died in The White Horse. There's a plaque.

KEVIN   I assure you not!

WILL   I've seen the plaque!

ERIC   (COMING FROM BEHIND THE BAR AND COLLECTING A PHOTO FROM THE WALL) Actually, he's right. He died outside that bar alright, but he was in here for the most of the night before.

KEVIN   (DOWNING THE DRINK) There 'tis!

ERIC   (HANDING THE PICTURE TO WILL) Signed this. Can't really make it out, mind. He was drunk. He was here from the time we opened the door to the time we closed, but my father, he ran the place at the time, knew he was in a bad way, so he made him go home. You know. Rather than kill one of the world's greatest poets.

WILL HANDS THE PICTURE BACK.

KEVIN   I was in Under Milk Wood once. 'Twas nine-teen seventy…

ERIC   Six.

KEVIN   Nineteen sixty-six! Cold winter. Horrible. I understudied for Burton (HE POINTS UP AGAIN) on these very boards.

WILL   Isn't it a play for voices?

KEVIN   True, true. You are most knowledgeable, my young friend. But what are actors if not voices on legs, mine own included. We are but the flesh and blood of another man's fingers as they run across the keyboard, hold the pen…

ERIC   Dictate into a machine I reckon it is nowadays.

WILL   (DISHEARTENED) You're actors.

KEVIN   (OFFERING HIS GLASS, WATCHING AS ERIC REFILLS IT WITHOUT ASKING, WHILE HE CRIBS STOPPARD) We are. At times. At times we are people, at times we are actors, though one scarcely knows the difference these days. (HE WINKS AT ERIC. HE'S FOUND A BENEFACTOR. ERIC HAS SET HIM UP WELL.)

WILL   (TO ERIC) You too?

ERIC Not as such. No. More of a stage hand. Yeah? Done a bit here and there, though.

KEVIN This man has raised the curtain on everyone from Aristophanes to Hare and drawn the curtain over many in-between. For flourish, beer or bourbon, he is your man. (HE DRINKS) Knows exactly when to raise it for a bow or draw it for a tomato, I assure you.

WILL You know, you have a very unique way of talking?

KEVIN You are most perspicacious, sirrah! 'Twas my mother that formed me thus. She was English. My father Gallic, though I know not what, and between them, a childhood in America, and more performances of Twelfth Night than I can count without blushing have made me what I am.

WILL (BITTER) Shakespeare.

KEVIN (HOLDING UP HIS GLASS FOR A REFILL QUICKLY AND GETTING ONE) You have quarrel with the bard, sir? It much becomes you.

WILL (DEFENSIVE) I like Shakespeare!

KEVIN And well you might!

WILL Know what the first play I saw was?

KEVIN & ERIC Midsummer Night's Dream.

WILL NODS SULLENLY

KEVIN (DRAWING OUT THE SCENE DRAMATI-CALLY) There you were. Central Park…

WILL (CORRECTING) Boston Common.

KEVIN (BARELY MISSING A BEAT) Boston Common. Sunset! The summer edging to a close. Sitting on your father's knee…

WILL I was fifteen.

KEVIN (WITHOUT BREAKING) The cusp of manhood ready to break in you. Art ready to fall upon you. Row on row of white chairs falling in the evening mist, looking for the world like Arlington at the end of the war.

WILL   Actually, it was freezing and my brother had a bong.

TIM IS STARING AT WILL.

ERIC   (SHRUGGING) Helps pass the time.

KEVIN   (BELOWING. WILL JUMPS.) "Now, fair Hippolyta, our nuptial hour draws on apace."

ERIC   (PUTTING ON A WOMAN'S VOICE) "Four days will quickly steep themselves in nights!"

KEVIN   Damn right they will!

THE PAIR GRIN AT EACH OTHER: THIS IS WHAT THEY LIVE FOR. WILL SLUMPS. WHAT HAS HE GOTTEN HIMSELF INTO?

ERIC   And you never knew, did you?

KEVIN   Before you were only of the screen. A pale two dimensions that repeated like…

ERIC   A bad case of déjà vu?

KEVIN   Touché!

ERIC   And you saw, what?

KEVIN   The full, fertile three dimensions, a breath rounded out. A word, performed, motivated… Acted!

WILL   Left after the interval.

TIM IS STARING AT WILL. HE GIVES HIM A WAVE.

KEVIN   The second act is tedious, I'll grant you that.

WILL   (TO KEVIN AND ERIC) Excuse me. (TO TIM) Can I help you?

ERIC   Ah, don't mind him.

WILL   He's staring at me.

ERIC   He doesn't speak. You know. He can't help it.

KEVIN   (TO TIM) Tim! Come! Join our merry crew. (BUT TIM JUST TURNS AWAY)

ERIC   (SOTTO) Lost his tongue some years back.

KEVIN   'Twas a foul deed.

ANNOYED, TIM GETS UP AND GOES TO THE BATHROOM.

ERIC   They offered to put it back and everything.

WILL   Who did?

ERIC   The doctors. Said they could do a lot with it, but they didn't.

WILL   Why not?

ERIC   Wouldn't let them.

KEVIN   'Twas a foul deed. But there it seems is where love will guide you! He was the best amongst us.

WILL   An actor?

ERIC   Best there was! Bound for stardom, some say. Not much to look at now, I'll give you that, but at the time they say he could turn the head of any girl, old or young.

KEVIN   I swear, I never saw him in a part that wasn't made for him. He was Troilus. He was Mark Antony. Once he'd played a character there was not one man in a thousand would touch it. I swear. A different man trod those boards every time. 'Twas as though his skin became the habit of a ghost. His countenance the play-wright's imagination!

ERIC   No kidding. He was good though! Saw him that final night. What was it?

KEVIN   Candida.

ERIC   That was it. He was Marchbanks. Candida was…

KEVIN   (PORTENTOUSLY) Grace Marceau.

ERIC   (IN WONDERMENT) Grace Marceau!

KEVIN   Best thighs in the business.

ERIC   When he came off, I remember this, I had the curtain. When he came off, at the end, after the speech…

KEVIN   "In a hundred years we shall be the same age. But I have a better secret than that in my heart. Let me go now. The night outside grows impatient."

ERIC   There was no sound of applause. Not a single clap in the house at all. Nothing!

KEVIN   Nothing!

ERIC   I lowered that curtain like it was a shroud. (HE HOLDS HIS HANDS UP) I know, I know. He's the one for words, but that's what it was like. A shroud. I lowered it and nothing.

KEVIN   And we waited.

ERIC   Five. Ten seconds, and not a sound.

KEVIN   Then it came.

ERIC   A single clap.

KEVIN   The sound of one hand clapping.

ERIC   (GIVING KEVIN A REPROACHFUL LOOK FOR SPOILING THE MOMENT) One man. That's all! And nothing else. We looked at each other, like you do. You know. In the wings. We looked at each other and Tim gave a shrug…

KEVIN   It was Marceau.

ERIC   And they went back on. Tim says to me…

KEVIN   Last words he ever spoke.

ERIC   "Pull it up, Eric." So I did. And the place shook with thunder like I've never heard before or since.

KEVIN   Nevermore!

ERIC   They forgot it was a play, see. That's how good he was. And it's not the kind of play you forget is a play, if you catch my drift.

ERIC   They were waiting for him in the alley after that.

WILL   They?

KEVIN   Them.

ERIC   See, you got to understand. Marcau, she was…

KEVIN   Well…

ERIC   Exactly.

KEVIN   So, what? He just stopped speaking?

ERIC   Well, once they'd cut out his tongue he did.

WILL   Jesus!

KEVIN   One does not, it seems, covet thy neighbour's moll.

WILL   Mafia?

ERIC   Doesn't pay to tell!

ABOVE THEIR HEADS THERE IS THE SOUND OF MUFFLED LAUGHTER FROM THE THEATRE AND WILL LOOKS UP.

KEVIN   You are, perhaps, thinking of rejoining?

WILL   No. No. I don't think so.

KEVIN   Yet it would seem there is something to draw you? (TO ERIC, WORRIED HE'S ABOUT TO LOSE HIS BENEFACTOR) Another, kind sir, if you so please!

WILL   (WHILE ERIC POURS THE DRINKS) I doubt it.

KEVIN   What know you of yonder divertissement?

WILL   (LISTENING TO THE SILENCE FROM UP-STAIRS) Huh?

ERIC   He means the play. You seem to, you know, care.

WILL   They're not laughing anymore.

KEVIN   And should they be?

WILL   (CHECKING HIS WATCH) Pretty much.

ENTER TIM STAGE UP

KEVIN AND ERIC EXCHANGE LOOKS. TIM RE-EN-TERS FROM THE BATHROOM AND TAKES HIS PLACE AT THE BAR, STILL WATCHING WILL.

KEVIN   ' Tis a good play, I think. If the sound of the actors doesn't reach but the audience does. It's the sign of, well, felicitude at least. Didn't happen to see a poster on the way in?

ERIC   Something about a radio, I think.

KEVIN   That's right! I heard it from somewhere. A name and a radio.

WILL   The Curse of Brian McArthur. The radio was on the poster. (HE SLUMPS IN HIS CHAIR) They should be laughing now.

KEVIN   (PORTENTOUSLY) I see.

ERIC   Another one, then? (WILL HOLDS UP HIS

GLASS. ERIC POURS) What's it about?

WILL   About two hours too long, it seems.

KEVIN   Ah. The curtain calls!

ERIC   Write or direct it?

WILL   Both.

ERIC   And now that they've signed you up with promises of fame and fortune you're left you dangling – that it?

WILL   Pretty much.

ERIC   Let me guess. Half the profits? Three week run? But…

KEVIN   Only if they get half the gate on opening night!

ERIC   Exactly.

WILL   (LOOKING FORLORN) The bastards.

ERIC   I wouldn't take it personally.

KEVIN   Old Scene-Cutter's a good one alright. He'll have you by the balls, and no mistake.

ERIC   Did you put money upfront?

WILL   Half.

ERIC   And the performance rights?

WILL   No.

KEVIN   Well! Then you should consider yourself lucky. I would. Many a man he's got the better of with that one!

ERIC   He's right, you know. Could have been worse.

WILL   You telling me I've been had?

UNSEEN BY WILL, TIM CASTS AN IMAGINARY FISHING LINE OVER THE BAR AND REELS ONE IN.

KEVIN   Hook, line, and sinker.

ERIC   Listen. You shouldn't be too hard on yourself. It happens to the best. Trust me. And you know, Scene-Cutter's just doing his job, really. Most plays we get in here… Well, of course, I don't mean yours… But most plays, they're – well, shit, you know? They're like, someone steps on stage and preaches something for three hours, or something. No one wants to see that.

KEVIN   No one should have to.

ERIC   What I'm saying is, Scene-Cutter's just doing his job. This theatre, it's been open since before the Depression. Real long. Most of the people here, most of the folks who come back, they want what they're used to. You catch my drift? They want…

WILL   Shakespeare?

ERIC   Usually, yeah. But we've got a reputation as a place for new talent. Wilde, Shaw…

KEVIN   (WITH CONTEMPT) Hare.

ERIC   Neil Simon. They all did their first stuff here. But then, you know that if you wrote the thing. So…

KEVIN   So old Scene-Cutter puts on a fresh face now and then. Bankrolls them, so to speak, and people think it avant-garde.

ERIC   They come, which is the point. And then they come back when something they really want to see is on.

KEVIN   It is the devil of the modern age.

ERIC   Market forces! Look at it this way. You've got your play performed, know what I mean? Got your name up in lights.

KEVIN   Well, not lights.

ERIC   No, not lights. But you know what I mean. Got your name up there. Got what you wanted. And don't take this the wrong way, but six months from now you're gonna be writing sitcoms for a thousand bucks an hour and no one's going to care about it. You're not going to care about it!

WILL   I will if I have to write sitcoms!

TIM COMES AROUND THE BAR AND RAPS ON THE TABLE. THE THREE LOOK AT HIM. TIM HOLDS HIS HANDS, FIRST TO HIS EARS, THEN TO HIS MOUTH, GESTURES TO WILL WITH ONE HAND AND BOWS, POLITELY.

ERIC   (TO TIM) Really?

KEVIN   Well, there we have it then! A drink for the bard! (WHEN NO ONE OFFERS HE LEANS OVER THE BAR, POURS HIMSELF ONE, DOWNS IT, AND POURS HIMSELF ANOTHER).

WILL   What?

ERIC   He says he likes your play. (TIM RAPS ON THE BAR) Loves it.

WILL   Really?

TIM GESTURES AGAIN, SLAPPING HIS CHEST AND GRIPPING HIS FIST BEFORE SMILING BROADLY AND THROWING WORDS FROM HIS MOUTH.

WILL (CONT.)   I'm sorry. I don't…

ERIC   He says you have a heart for dialogue. Beautiful, you are, he says. (TIM STAMPS HIS FOOT) With words.

TIM GESTURES A MASK ON HIS FACE AND THEN SIGHS.

ERIC (CONT.)   Though the actors are crap.

WILL   (TAKEN ABACK BY THIS) Thank you. I mean, really. (HE LOOKS AT TIM CAREFULLY AND SPEAKS MORE CLEARLY AS THOUGH HE IS DEAF) Thank you!

TIM NODS AND HEADS BACK TO HIS SIDE OF THE BAR.

KEVIN   And he rarely says but one word about anything, too.

ERIC   (TAKING THE BOTTLE BACK OFF KEVIN) Wish I'd seen it now. He watches the rehearsals, you know. Old Scene-Cutter can hardly throw him out and he's as quiet as a mouse, (TO TIM) aren't you?

TIM COVERS HALF HIS FACE AND SIPS HIS DRINK WITH A SMILE.

ERIC   Our very own Phantom. So what's it about, this play of yours?

WILL   Look I really am touched. Really. It's nice to know. But all I know is that this is a year of my life and half my savings out the window for what's turned out to be a one-night vanity piece.

KEVIN   Tish and piffle! Come. We must have it.

ERIC   Come on. What's it going to hurt?

WILL   Thank you. Really. It's kind of you, but it doesn't stop it being a flop!

ERIC   You can't think of it like that. Really. You can't think of it like that.

KEVIN   It's the cost of business. Some pay, others pay for it, but it costs us all in the end, no matter what we gain!

ERIC   Who knows. There's always people here. Maybe it'll get a movie or something. Or put on somewhere else.

WILL   What? Like a high school? And anyway, I don't want a movie. I don't…

KEVIN   Who would want staccatos when they can have ariettas? Who sex when they can have romance ? Who…

ERIC   Video games when you still have a life.

KEVIN   And who a movie when you can have (IN AWE) the stage.

ERIC   He's right.

TIM NODS.

WILL   I like movies.

KEVIN   Don't we all!

WILL   It's just that…

KEVIN   You didn't write flesh and blood to see it turned into a photograph.

WILL   Exactly! I like plays. I love plays. (HE POINTS TO THE STAGE ABOVE HIM.) To see that up there. The rounding out of a character. Becoming the words! Knowing that if you were to do it again it would be different because you are different than you were the last time you did it! To put words into the mouths of other people.

That's what I wanted here!

KEVIN   (CLAPPING HIM ON THE SHOULDER)

Ah, a poet! Truly the bard lives on! (HE HOLDS OUT HIS GLASS) Drink! (AS ERIC POURS) Let me tell you young…

WILL   Will.

KEVIN   Young Will! The theatre is the last bastion of art in human form. Nowhere else, especially not in movies, does man take the form of art – not artist, art! – but on the stage. Who gives two penneths what it looks like when you can do a take a thousand times. Art, if nothing else, is transcendence, and there is no transcendence in repeating a line until you get it right, is there? (HE HOLDS UP HIS NEWLY FILLED GLASS) Cheers.

WILL   All I know is that my play – be it funny, be it poignant, be it sacrilege – is getting scrapped so that them up there (HE POINTS TO THE ROOF) can get A Midsummer Night's Dream on in the middle of November! A play, I might add, that they've seen a thousand times already. That they know. That they can bloody well chant, line for line!

ERIC   People want what they've always wanted. I'm sorry, man. I'm all for new plays, but there's not a theme that's not been done to death. Why listen to someone else talking about something you already know when there's someone you know who tells it better.

ENTER SAM AND BOB.

A COUPLE, SAM AND BOB, AUDIENCE MEMBERS FROM THE THEATRE ABOVE, COME DOWN THE STAIRS INTO THE BAR. THEY ARE DRESSED IN A TUX AND A BALLGOWN. BOTH APPEAR AFFLUENT. BOB IS IN HIS LATE FIFTIES. HIS WIFE, SAM, IS A BEAUTIFUL TWENTY-SOMETHING.

BOTH ARE QUITE DRUNK. SAM SLIPS ON THE

STEP AND BOB CATCHES HER. BOTH LAUGH.
THEY HURRY INTO THE ROOM AND HEAD FOR
THE BAR.
AT THE INTRUSION THE THREE AT THE BAR
DROP INTO WHISPERS.
KEVIN   (SOTTO) What my friend is trying to say, in
his own patulous way, is that there is nothing new under
heaven.
ERIC   (SOTTO) And why listen to someone new tell
you the story when an old friend can do the same!
KEVIN   (SOTTO) Exactly!
THE THREE FALL SILENT AND PART FOR THE
TWO DRUNKEN INTERLOPERS. BOB RAPS ON THE
BAR FOR SERVICE.

Scene II – The Patron

BOB   Drink!

ERIC   What will it be?

BOB   JD and cola for the lady and… Umm, what have you got in terms of pure malt Scotch?

ERIC   Glenmorangie…

BOB   Excellent. Drank it at the Open last year. Good enough for Tiger, good enough for me, eh?

ERIC   Right you are.

ERIC GOES TO POUR THE DRINKS. THE PAIR SLUMP ONTO THE STOOLS.

BOB   (TO THE BAR AT LARGE) You guys escaped it too, eh? Should never have gone back up after the break, if you ask me. Not exactly Romeo and Juliet, if you catch my drift.

SAM   The lead actor was quite good!

BOB   Was he? Who can tell. All that one-flew-over-the-cuckoo's-nest. Who wants that nowadays?

WILL (SARCASTICALLY) And what do you want?

BOB   (MISSING THE SARCASM) Well, I'll tell you. We want murder, intrigue, and a little bit of lust, if you know what I mean.

SAM   Darling!

BOB   No, I said it! Sex, blood, and… (HE CAN'T THINK OF ANY MORE) more sex, or more blood. Anyway, none of this talking to the damn audience, dammit. Would Pacino talk to the damn audience? I think not.

WILL (ANGRY) "Looking for Richard."

SAM   Didn't like that. I don't do documentaries, you know. Where's the escape?

BOB   Now that's what we need more of: Shakespeare!

WILL Jesus!

BOB Boy knew how to write a damn play, I'll give him that! Can't understand half of what he's saying, but then that's the point, right?

SAM And the costumes are so lovely.

BOB There's got to be… I don't know… Something unreal about a play. These kids these days don't seem to get that, you know? All these dream sequences.

SAM And the romance!

WILL Oberon was a member of the Senate, was he?

BOB What?

SAM I just like the dresses, is all!

KEVIN What my good friend here is trying to say is that even the immortal bard…

WILL Jesus!

KEVIN (NOT MISSING A BEAT) …the Aristotelian muse, had to perform his work for the first time somewhere!

SAM Oh, I saw that!

KEVIN Even myths must have their momentum.

SAM Gwyneth Paltrow and whatshisname?

ERIC We were all young once.

SAM The English guy with the sexy eyes?

BOB And I'm all for it, you know? I'm a goddamned season ticket holder here! Box and everything! Even though it is half price. (WILL HANGS HIS HEAD) I'm all for supporting the arts.

SAM 'Long as we don't have to sit through them.

BOB Amen! Barkeep?

ERIC POURS HIM ANOTHER.

BOB That's the spot.

WILL So what you're saying is, new plays are pointless!

BOB Boy, everything that was said was said in the five plays of Shakespeare. Everything else is a copy. That, and the Bible.

THE ROOM IS SILENT.

ERIC   Five plays?

BOB   Oh, I know some say he didn't write all of them, but who cares? They're the five plays! One man wrote them, five men wrote them. Same goddamn thing, if you ask me.

SILENCE.

KEVIN   Out of curiosity, my good sir. What pray are the five plays?

BOB   Hey, you're British aren't you?

KEVIN   For my sins.

BOB   Then you should know! Midsummer Night. Hamlet.

SAM   Romeo and Juliet.

BOB   Macbeth and King Lear.

SAM   And that one they made into a movie, what was the title?

BOB   Oh, ok. I see what you're getting at. Six. Alright. Excuse me! That one with the black actor, whatshisname.

SAM   Denzel Day Lewis.

BOB   That's the man!

WILL   Much Ado About Nothing.

BOB   What?

KEVIN   (SUDDENLY TAKING UMBRAGE.) Sir, I must tell you that there are thirty-eight plays by the bard!

WILL   Thirty-nine.

KEVIN   Thirty-nine!

WILL   The Rape of Lucrece.

KEVIN   And I have trod the boards with them all!

SAM   I thought that was in the Second World War?

BOB   Alright! Alright! Jesus. Of course there are more! I meant five good ones.

ERIC   Six.

BOB   Six.

SAM   In China?

BOB   I'm just saying that if you want theatre done, do Shakespeare. I mean, that's why we sat through it in high school, right!

SAM   Or was it Italy? Berlusconi.

BOB   I'm saying that. "To be or not to be." "An eye for an eye and a tooth for a tooth." And all that.

WILL   Actually, that's from the Bible. Which is funny, because when I was young, my parents, they're pretty religious, and my mother used to quote Bible verses to me all the time. You know, when I was bad or something. She'd say something like "cleanliness is next to godliness – that's in the Bible." Or "neither a borrower nor a lender be – that's in the Bible." Then I grew up and found out they were Shakespeare's.

BOB   And what do you do, young man?

WILL   I'm a playwright.

BOB   (INTERESTED) Really? You should submit something. I'm a custodian here and I can see it gets on. Would I have seen any of your work?

WILL   You'd have walked out during the second act. That's my play on upstairs.

THERE IS SILENCE.

SAM   The lead actor was handsome!

BOB   Well. Ain't I the schmuck, I guess. Excuse me for my opinions. Who am I to judge, right? I mean, I just made sixty million bucks last year and kept this hole open! Sorry I'm not arty enough for you!

WILL   Apparently I'd have to be dead five hundred years for you to like me.

BOB   You know, screw you! All that talking at the audience!

WILL   What, you mean like a narrator?

KEVIN "Two Households, both alike in dignity. In fair Verona where we lay our scene."

BOB Ok. Ok. I get it. But that dialogue, man. All that… If I want to hear how the man in the street talks I'd rent a rap video! Come on! Where's the poetry?

SAM Where's the romance?

WILL He's sixty-five!

BOB Who is?

WILL (POINTING UPWARDS) Brian MacArthur! The character! What do you want from him!

SAM Romance doesn't stop at twenty!

BOB Sure it does, honey. Look. I'm sorry we didn't like your play, alright. If I'd have known you wrote it I'd have been nicer about it, you know?

SAM And you could have done something with the dresses!

BOB But what I want, and let me tell you, what I want is what everyone wants. Everyone who can afford a ticket that is, what… (WILL LOOKS AWAY) What? You think that's Joe Public in the cheap seats up there? Joe Public don't give a damn about theatre! Joe Public don't like to dress up, and you got to dress up for the theatre. Joe public wants to eat pizza off his goddamned chest in bed watching reruns of Friends on TV, that's what Joe public wants. What we want is a bit of culture! We don't want to be educated about no goddamned street car. We don't want no… exposition on the world today. Shit, that's why we buy Forbes! We want to put our education to use and our education is, was, and goddamned always will be William-fucking-Shakespeare! We want lines we don't understand. We want plot holes so big you can drive a truck through them. We want to make sense of it all! Or at least understand what we studied it for in the first place! You want to put on a play? We want Shakespeare!

WILL   I'm a writer, not a director!

BOB   Then write a goddamned Shakespeare play. Fucked if any of us would know the difference. Drink!

BOB HOLDS UP HIS GLASS AND ERIC POURS AS THE ROOM STAYS SILENT.

BOB (CONT.) And I'll tell you another thing! I didn't sit through fucking hours of Keats and couplets and crap and what have you so I could buy and sell commodities. No! I sat through it so when I did, I'd be accepted into society, know what I mean? Now that I'm here, the last thing I wanna hear on stage is people who talk like me!

WILL   (EXASPERATED) I can't... So if I want to write plays, I have to write like a dead man?

BOB   Why the hell not! Let me tell you kid. Everything's commercial. Everything! It's all about money, and most of it's about mine. You give the people what they want and they thank you for it. You want to make a living, suck up and do sonnets!

KEVIN   My friend, it is clear to me that you know nothing about art, and less still about theatre. Art is expression. It is creative! Acting is putting flesh and blood to the animal of the imagination. Bones to words! We all lie in our own darkness and shout at the stars, hoping they can hear us, wondering if they can answer! The theatre, and dare I say art – nay, acting – is the very call of humanity. One cannot just write Shakespeare! Shakespeare is! One cannot simply create Antony, or Cleopatra. They are Platonic forms, existing since time immemorial within the consciousness of man, and expressed, imparted to us by the bard! We are all under his shadow, it is true. We all find our skies dotted with his cloud. But write Shakespeare? A man could no more breathe words than he could again Ophelia! Or Brutus. Katharina!

SAM   Who?

WILL   Kiss me Kate.

SAM   (WITH A SEXY POUT) My name's Sam.

ERIC   (POURING INTO KEVIN'S GLASS) Have a drink.

KEVIN SITS, EXHAUSTED INTO HIS SEAT AND DRINKS.

BOB   You don't know what you're talking about! You think everyone's like you? Let me tell you, friend. Nobody gives a shit about art until we're told to. No one has the faintest goddamned opinion! Hell, I read in a newspaper that you're the latest Van Gogh and I'll believe it, but till then you're nothing! Who chooses? Is that art? (HE POINTS UP) Is this!

SAM   I like paintings myself. And dresses. Ruffs! I like a bit of ruff.

SAM LAUGHS AT HER OWN JOKE. NO ONE JOINS IN.

WILL   (WILL IS THINKING) Still, it's interesting, isn't it.

ERIC   What is?

WILL   "Had I the heavens' embroidered cloths."

KEVIN Yeats.

WILL   (GESTURING TO BOB) Yeah, but who'd know, right? When Phantom of the Opera is the pinnacle of high society, who can tell what art is anymore. Let alone who made it! He can't.

BOB   Hey, I'm the one who buys the tickets, yeah? I've been working my goddamned guts out for the past thirty years. I'm not dumb!

WILL   (WAVING HIM OFF) No. Of course not. I didn't mean…

ERIC   So?

WILL   So, who would know? Really. Who could tell? Put together a vaguely Shakespearian theme. Throw in a few couplets. I doubt you'd even have to do it in iambic pentameter. Who'd know?

ERIC   You mean, write Shakespeare?

BOB   People want what they want! Be it O.J. or moon landings. Truth of it doesn't matter. Only that we believe it! A liar's not a liar if everyone thinks it's true.

SAM   I get bored with the same thing over and over again. But as long as they change the costumes…

WILL   You know, I'm half inclined to do it. I mean, imagine! A new play by William Shakespeare, performed here? It'd run for weeks and then…

KEVIN   You can't be serious?

TIM GETS UP, SLAPPING THE BAR.

BOB   (SHOCKED) Mary mother of Christ! Where'd he come from?

TIM WALKS AROUND THE BAR, SIDESTEPPING BOB AND SAM WHO, IN TURN, LOOK AT HIM WITH INCREDULITY AND A HINT OF DESIRE. HE STOPS BEFORE WILL, SMILES AT HIM, THE VERY SYMBOL OF CONFIDENCE, AND NODS. WILL SMILES BACK.

KEVIN   It can't be done! There is no one to hold a candle to…

ERIC   You know, I remember my brother coming to sec me after one production. Got here early. Ibsen play. Even watched the whole of the final act from the wings with me. Know what he said to me? "Shakespeare then, is it?"

BOB   What I've been saying! I'm not kidding, kid. You write a Shakespeare play. Make sure it's got lots of blood and sex. You know, like the old ones. And I'll help you put it on.

KEVIN   Madness!

WILL   It would have to be… timeless. The plot.

SAM   A King! There's always a King.

ERIC   Which kings did he do?

WILL   Richard.

TIM HOLDS UP THREE FINGERS, THEN TWO.

ERIC   Henry.

TIM HOLDS UP FIRST FOUR, THEN FIVE, THEN SIX THEN EIGHT FINGERS.

ERIC   They weren't any good though.

KEVIN   (DISPARAGING) Weren't any good?!

ERIC   Well, the fifth was good.

KEVIN   "Once more unto the breach." "Board up the holes with our English dead." Not bad, was it?

BOB   Don't have to be real. Doubt there was no Lear.

TIM STAMPS HIS FOOT.

WILL   No, he's right. It would have to be real. Otherwise the plot would be new to them. Something they know. Something… Something they'd think Shakespeare wrote in the first place.

ERIC   Henry the eighth, then?

WILL   But he did write it.

ERIC   Never seen it performed.

KEVIN   "Give her a hundred marks. I'll to the Queen!"

WILL   No. He wrote it. The point would be to do something he didn't write.

TIM MAKES THE FACE OF A LION.

ERIC   Richard the Lionheart!

WILL   Richard the Lionheart?

BOB   I've heard of him!

WILL   But then there's all that fighting in the Middle East. Too political. You know what they say about Shylock.

KEVIN   Blasphemy!

SAM   (TO ERIC) Excuse me? Ladies' room?

ERIC   (POINTING TO A DOOR) Over there, sweetheart. Call if there's no roll.

BOB   Nobody's gonna see an anti-Semitic play.

KEVIN   Sacrilege.

WILL   Where does that leave us?

THEY PAUSE IN THOUGHT. SAM GOES INTO THE BATHROOM

EXIT SAM STAGE LEFT

ERIC   How about his father?

WILL   I'm sorry, I'm not totally familiar with the Plantagenets.

KEVIN   (SULLENLY) Henry Plantagenet? Henry the second!

BOB   What did he do?

KEVIN   (ROUNDING ON HIM) Do? Do?! Nothing! I mean, king at seventeen, and not from the line either! Married the most beautiful woman and, I may add, the wife of his rival, the King of France! Killed his best friend! Do? Oh, not much at all!

BOB   Son, there ain't nobody I let speak to me like that!

KEVIN   Then you should be happy, for I am, indeed, a nobody.

BOB   Got that right.

KEVIN   In your world!

ERIC   Lads!

WILL   Thomas Becket! I'd forgotten about that!

ERIC   That's right. Had him killed in his own Cathedral.

WILL   The Lion in Winter! Peter O'Toole and Katherine Hepburn.

BOB   Hey, I saw that on TV! That guy from Star Trek and Glen whatshisname! That wasn't Shakespeare?

KEVIN   What? One of his five plays?

BOB   Listen friend. You ain't got something to say, why don't you say nothing.

KEVIN   A rhetorical statement in more than one effect.

WILL   Thomas Becket! Henry the Second! You might

have it there.

ERIC   Has all the hallmarks of a Shakespeare play. Love. Death.

BOB   Sex and blood?

WILL   Why not.

KEVIN (BESIDE HIMSELF AND FORGETTING ABOUT HIS NEED FOR PATRONAGE) Why not? I'll tell you why not! He didn't bloody write it is why not! And it's Saint Thomas Becket.

ERIC   Not then it wasn't.

KEVIN   It will never work!

WILL   Why not?

KEVIN   Because, my young friend, you are not Shakespeare – that's why not! You wouldn't know the first thing about writing in verse.

BOB   Doesn't have to be in verse. Just got to sound, you know, Shakespearian. Thee's and thou's and everything.

KEVIN   And that's what it is to you, is it? That's what it is? Difficult English?

BOB   That's what it is to everyone!

KEVIN   Henry didn't even kill Saint Thomas…

ERIC   He had people kill him.

KEVIN   No. No! He said "I wish he was dead," and his knights, who wanted him dead, took it literally!

BOB   Well, what's more Shakespearean than that?

WILL   (TO KEVIN) I don't see what your problem is here. We're just talking!

KEVIN   About rewriting history! About stealing a soul, another man's soul, for your own gain. Plagiarism!

WILL   It's not plagiarism if he didn't write it.

KEVIN   (EXASPERATED) Necrophilia then!

WILL   (A LITTLE ANGRY NOW) You don't get it, do you?

KEVIN   You never steal from another. That, my young

friend, is the rule above all. It is the creed! The flagon! The right in the writer!

WILL   (WOOING KEVIN) Don't… Don't you want to get back at them? Don't you still have something to prove? I mean, here you are, veteran of a thousand nights, but when did the spotlight shine for you. (POINTING AT ERIC) When did he pull the curtain on your call?

KEVIN   Hubris, the lot of it.

WILL   (TRYING TO APPEASE HIM) Come on! You are one of the greatest actors of our time! You are Mephistopheles! You are Lear! You are… (HE STRUGGLES)

ERIC   Agamemnon.

WILL   Agamemnon.

KEVIN   Well, Sir Toby Belch usually.

WILL   But (HE POINTS UPWARDS AND BEHIND) They reject you. Here you are, in your prime…

KEVIN   Boy, you are wasting your time. You are a good lad, and Tim feels something of a writer, I'll grant you that. But the Bard? The immortal Bard? I'm sorry. And not much of a flatterer either.

WILL   Don't you want to see something put over all those people in the cheap seats. All the people who'd pay for Romeo but never for Cressida? For Falstaff but not for Caliban? Wouldn't you like, just once, to see old Scene-Cutter on his knees, begging for something – you – to be put on? Begging you to be in something! I can see it now. "We turn then to England green."

KEVIN   See, you can't even do that! "We turn then to England green!"

WILL   How would it go then? If Shakespeare… if the Bard did it?

KEVIN   Well, he wouldn't use green for England for a start.

ENTER SARAH.
SARAH ENTERS FROM THE MAIN DOOR AND
LOOKS DOWN ON THE SCENE WITH GROWING
ANGER.
WILL   What would he use?
KEVIN   Pale green.
ERIC   We turn to England pale green.
KEVIN   (IMPERIOUS) Turn we then to pale England's
green!'
EVERYONE CLAPS.
SARAH   What the hell is going on?

Scene III – The Wife

THE ILLUSION IS BROKEN BY SARAH'S ARRIVAL
AS SHE COMES DOWN THE STAIRS TOWARDS
WILL.

ERIC   (SHOCKED) What can I get you, sweetheart?

WILL   Sarah!

KEVIN   (INCENSED) Madam! Do you mind!

BOB   (COMING BACK TO THE BAR) Fun while it
lasted.

KEVIN   You have driven away the eternal muse!

SARAH IGNORES KEVIN AND HEADS TOWARDS
WILL.

SARAH   (ACCUSING) I thought you were backstage!

WILL   We were kind of in…

KEVIN   You know this woman?

SARAH   This woman happens to be married to this
man, if you don't mind.

KEVIN   Your wife?

WILL   For better or worse.

KEVIN   (CHANGING HIS TONE COMPLETELY TO
ONE OF CHARM) Dear madam! May I…

SARAH   (IGNORING HIM) Honey? This is your day!
What the hell are you doing in the bar?

BOB   (TURNING BACK TO THE BAR) Ah well.

WILL   I needed some air, that's all.

SARAH   Alcohol is more like it. I don't understand you,
I really don't. I mean, this is your day! Really. This is what
we've worked for. This is your big break and you're down
here with, what? The rejects from Fame? (TO BOB) No
offence.

BOB   I was thinking much the same.

WILL   Listen…

SARAH   Weren't you listening? They love it! I mean, I don't know much about plays, you know that, darling, but really, this is your moment! We're near the end and…

WILL   It doesn't matter.

KEVIN   Madam, if I may?

SARAH   (TURNING ON KEVIN) If you don't mind, I'm trying to have a word with my husband! I'm sure that the barman will serve you with whatever you thought my husband was buying. Out of your own pocket!

KEVIN OPENS HIS MOUTH AND SHUTS IT AGAIN. DUMBFOUNDED, HE MOVES AWAY, BROKEN. ONLY TIM REMAINS WATCHING. THE REST LOOK AWAY, GOING ABOUT THEIR OWN BUSINESS.

WILL   Honey…

SARAH   What?

WILL   It's a con.

SARAH   What is?

WILL   This. The play. It's… They put on a new play every now and again, but half the seats out there are free. There's no way we'll take enough.

SARAH   I don't… This is opening night!

WILL   There's… There's a clause in the contract. If we don't fill half the seats, if we can't take half the house, the play closes.

SARAH   But it's a full house. Don't be silly…

WILL   It's a con. Those are all season ticket holders, like this guy here.

BOB   He's right, I'm afraid. I wouldn't pay a penny to watch a new play, no offence.

WILL   None taken.

SARAH   But, surely…

BOB   We all get an invite. New production. Free tickets. It makes us feel like patrons of the arts, see?

ERIC Only, there's no new play. Not really. They just put it on.

SARAH But we've got two weeks?

WILL Only if we can half fill the house.

SARAH But it's full!

WILL But nobody's paid. Well…

SARAH (REALISING) And the money we put up?

ERIC That's the con, I'm afraid. They've been rehearsing Midsummer's for the past month, ready to go on tomorrow. Still from all the sounds of it, your man here has got the gift. Really. I think he'll be able to do his own thing next time. You know, The John Wilkes Booth Memorial Theatre, Minnesota or something. Probably get it up front.

SARAH You said we'd get that back!

WILL They told me it was full! They said…

SARAH (EXPLODING) So, what? You telling me we put our savings into this for, what? Nothing? A one-night fucking thing? Jesus!

WILL Darling…

SARAH Jesus! I mean. Jesus!

WILL Darling…

SHE IS READY TO BLOW AND THE REST OF THE CAST TURN AWAY.

SARAH I don't believe it! Fuck! I mean… Jesus! How can you be so dumb! Really! How can you be so fucking dumb all the fucking time! Jesus.

WILL (EMBARRASSED) Come on!

SARAH Jesus!

WILL Hey, I'm as pissed as you are but…

SARAH No, you're not pissed! You're (SHE MOTIONS TO THE BAR) Pissed!

WILL Come on!

SARAH Well, that's it then!

WILL   Come on!

SARAH   No, that's it! Over.

WILL   (GETTING UP) Look, let's talk about it…

SARAH   You talk about it. I'm going.

WILL   Come on!

SARAH   Screw you.

EXIT SARAH UPSTAGE.

WILL SITS DOWN AGAIN. THE BAR IS SILENT. ABOVE THEM THE SOUND OF APPLAUSE WAFTS DOWN THROUGH THE CEILING. THE PLAY IS OVER.

ERIC   (MOVING AROUND THE BAR) Better get this lot cleared up then.

BOB   (TO WILL) That's some woman.

WILL   Yeah.

BOB   And I know women.

SAM   She's very pretty.

BOB   Hell of a mouth on her. No offence.

WILL   Yeah.

BOB   I had a woman like that once. Broke my heart. Broke my balls! Cracked them in two. (HE GESTURES) Like that! Woman like that can take your balls with nothing more than a glance, am I right?

SAM   I thought she was pretty.

BOB   (TO SAM) Course you did honey. (TO WILL, ABOUT SAM) Heart the size of Manhattan. (ABOUT SARAH) Woman like that, heart the size of a nut. Heart the size of the balls she'll rip off you. Am I right?

WILL   (GETTING UP TO LEAVE AND PUTTING MONEY ON THE TABLE) Yeah, whatever.

BOB   (PICKS UP THE MONEY AND STUFFS IT BACK INTO WILL'S HAND, AND MOVES IN CLOSE) Listen to me. I'm trying to tell you something! Listen! There are only two types of women, son. Partners, my young naïve friend. Those with you for you. Those who just want to spend time with you because you're such a goddamned interesting person to be around. And those who are with you for themselves! You need to ask yourself this. Which one is she?

WILL (TRYING TO BREAK AWAY) I've got to go.

BOB (BLOCKING HIM) Because a woman like that is with you for only one reason, and that's to bring you down! To bring you down so she can be up! You're either gold or dirt. Nothing inbetween.

SAM Honey?

BOB And as soon as you're one, she'll want to make you the other.

SAM Honey!

WILL Let me go.

BOB (MOVING BACK) Hey, go! Fuck! I'm not standing in your way. But ask yourself this. Where you going to, son? To that? Because there's nothing there that's not designed to fuck you.

SAM Darling…

BOB (TURING TO SAM) Now this here. This is gold! I mean it! Why you think she's with me?

WILL (OFFERING THE MONEY TO ERIC) This enough?

BOB (INTERCEPTING) You think it's the money, don't you? You think she's with me for the cash?

WILL (ANGRY) Alright, yes.

BOB She's with me cos I'm rich?

WILL Yes!

BOB Pretty girl like this. Only with me for the greenbacks!

SAM Stop it!

WILL Why else!

BOB 'Atta boy. You think she's fucking me, hoping my

heart runs out. That it? She just closes her eyes and thinks of Lincoln!

WILL   Something like that. Yes.

BOB   Ah, now there's teeth. Good boy!

WILL   (TURNING BACK TO THE BAR) Money's on the bar, alright.

BOB   (TAKING THE MONEY, HE GRABS WILL BY THE COLLAR AND STUFFS THE MONEY VIOLENTLY IN HIS POCKET) Don't you get it? Your money's no good here! Not upstairs, not down!

WILL   What do you want from me?!

BOB   I don't want anything from you! I've got everything. I've got money falling out of my ass. I've got a beautiful woman on my arm…

WILL   Look, I'm sorry.

BOB   You don't have to apologise. You're right! Your mistake is you think my money and me aren't the same thing.

WILL   What?

BOB   I die, and I will die, and every penny she spends will remind her of me because I am my money! I am! Money is success and I am every goddamn red cent of it. It's who I am! Fuck me! I must be a success! Now who the fuck are you?

WILL   (ANGRY) They ripped me off! Don't you get that! I promised her this!

BOB   You promised her shit!

WILL   I promised her this! This! This is what I was working for. This is what we put our money into! Don't tell me what I promised her. I promised her this!

BOB   And you got fucked! Want to go home and get fucked again? That what you want? You've got the talent. She knows that! You know that! Fuck, what you were doing here…

WILL   You want me to fake Shakespeare?

BOB   I want you to be a man! Be a man! (WILL LOOKS OFF ANGRILY) What? I bet she's got a nice job lined up for you, right? Balls in a sack over daddy's mantelpiece? Nine to five in a hardware store while her family says told-you-so. That it?

WILL   It's not as easy as all that!

BOB   Sure it is. You're you and she's there for you, or you're hers and she's there for her. (GESTURING TO THE BAR) You do this. You do it so well that I can't tell the from thee and I'll bankroll you.

THE REST OF THE BAR, EXCEPT SAM, LOOK ON IN INTEREST. EVEN KEVIN'S SPIRITS RISE.

WILL   (SHOCKED) You'd put up the money?

BOB   I'd pay for it!

WILL   Why? I mean, for what? Nobody would know!

BOB   Why not? Fuck 'em. Put it on, then tell them. Hey, schmucks, I wrote this. I did this you bunch of sycophantic, head-up-your-own-ass snotnoses. Look at me! Or take the cash and run with it. Up to you.

WILL   You're nuts!

BOB   You write it. Give it to my good friend here… (HE POINTS AT ERIC.)

ERIC   Eric.

BOB   …Eric and he'll give it to me. It fools me and I'll put it on. Full run. See if the fuckers can tell shit from shilola!

KEVIN   If it fooled even one critic it would be… (HE LEAVES THE THOUGHT DANGLING.)

BOB   There, see! You got yourself a cast. You got yourself an idea. Now get me a script!

WILL   Why you doing this?

BOB   Because sometimes we are not our situations. The best painter never picked up a brush. The best musician died at birth. And the best fucking men get their balls cut off by women. Go prove her wrong!

WILL   How long have I got?

BOB   I give a shit?

ERIC   There's a hole in the schedule about three months from now. Two week run.

BOB   There you are then.

WILL   That's not long enough…

BOB   Go.

WILL   You're nuts. You know that.

BOB   Go.

WILL STOPS AND LOOKS AT THE PEOPLE AROUND HIM.

BOB   (CONT.) Go!

THE CAST WATCH HIM AS HE GOES UP THE STAIRS. AT THE TOP HE TURNS TO LOOK AT THEM AGAIN, THEN EXITS.

EXIT WILL.

SAM   Honey…

BOB   We'll go in minute. (TO KEVIN) You're quiet.

KEVIN   I am.

BOB   (PULLING ON HIS COAT) Think he can do it?

KEVIN   He has it in him. Aye.

BOB   And they'll believe it?

KEVIN   Maybe. Yes. Some of them will. You have a plan?

BOB   Something like that.

KEVIN   Concerning, may I ask?

BOB   Money. Of course. What else. (HE PULLS A CARD OUT OF HIS WALLET AND PUTS IT ON THE TABLE) Let me know when he comes back, and send me the tab for drinks till now. (KEVIN REACHES OUT AND PULLS THE BOTTLE TOWARDS HIMSELF) That too.

BOB AND SAM HEAD TOWARDS THE DOOR. TIM

STEPS FORWARD, EXTENDS A HAND IN FRIEND-
SHIP.

BOB (CONT.) You're a great actor, son. (TAKING IT)
Better hope Shakespeare wrote a mute into his cast.

EXIT BOB AND SAM UPSTAGE.

CURTAINS.

END OF ACT I.

ACT II

The Writer

CURTAINS OPEN ON WILL'S OFFICE.
AN ATTIC CONVERTED INTO A WRITER'S OFFICE,
IT IS A PEAKED ROOM, HIGH AT THE CENTRE,
WITH WOODEN BEAMS SLOPING DOWN TO
REACH THE FLOOR ON EITHER SIDE. IN THE CEN-
TRE OF THE ROOM ON THE FAR WALL, ABOVE A
DESK AND MISMATCHED CHAIR THAT IS DECO-
RATED WITH A LONE COMPUTER, A NOTEPAD,
AND A PEN, IS A SMALL OVAL WINDOW FROM
WHICH LIGHT FALLS IN ONTO THE PINE WOOD-
EN FLOOR.
CENTRE STAGE AN OPEN TRAP DOOR LETS IN A
SHAFT OF LESS NATURAL LIGHT IN FROM BELOW,
A LADDER STRETCHING UP THROUGH IT.
THE SIDES OF THE ROOM ARE COVERED WITH
SHELFLESS BOOKS.
IN THE CENTRE OF THE ROOM A LOW-SWUNG
BARE LIGHT BULB, HANGS FROM THE CEILING.
ENTER FOOL.
FOOL Turn then, night to day and bar to home
At his desk the writer, all alone,
Must summon up the Theban muse
Or all his hopes and dreams, he'll lose.

ENTER WILL, EMERGING FROM THE TRAP DOOR,
A COFFEE CUP IN ONE HAND. HE MAKES HIS WAY
TO THE COMPUTER, SITS – HIS BACK TO US –
AND, PLACING THE COFFEE BY THE SIDE OF THE

COMPUTER, OPENS A WORD PROCESSING DOCU-
MENT.

He comes, bent, broken, spirits sank –
He's interviewed for CitiBank.
For wife wants him to bend in awe
To the money of father-in-law.
He must type, he must, on pages mute
Or end up working in a suit.
If a tie is not to make his noose
The immortal bard he must set loose.

EXIT FOOL .

WILL   (TO HIMSELF) Okay. Come on. Where was I?

HE SCANS THE DOCUMENT FOR A MOMENT
AND THEN STARTS TYPING, READING OUT THE
WORDS AS HE DOES SO.

WILL   Act two, scene three. Enter King Henry.

HE STOPS TYPING AND LEANS BACK, IMAGINING
THE SCENE.

DRESSED AS KING HENRY, TIM ENTERS FROM
THE WINGS AND PAUSES, FROZEN IN POSITION
WHILE WILL WONDERS WHAT TO DO WITH
HIM. A PROJECTION OF WILL'S IMAGINATION, HE
DOESN'T MOVE UNTIL WILL STARTS TO WRITE.
WILL STARTS TYPING.

TIM   Light! God's light!

WILL   Enter… (HE PAUSES, UNABLE TO THINK OF
A NAME) Err, placename.

ENTER ERIC DRESSED AS A SERF, A FLAMING
TORCH IN HIS HAND.

ERIC   My liege!

TIM   Good… (HE FREEZES)

WILL   (THINKING) Placename.

TIM   (UNFREEZING) What have you for me?

ERIC   The gods' light, my liege.

TIM   (AMUSED) Would that it shine brighter. 'Tis God's light I seek, not light of the gods.

ERIC   (CONFUSED) My liege?

TIM   'Tis heaven that vexes me thus, not aged eyes.

ERIC   (TURNING TO GO) My liege.

TIM   Stay. Hark you this? Are you mine?

ERIC   My lord?

TIM   My servant?

ERIC   Most trusted one, I warrant, my lord.

TIM   You have the shape of him. But have you this….

WILL   (WITHOUT PAUSE) Placename.

TIM   Have you friendship?

ERIC   To think as so, aye my lord.

TIM   Deep as blood. As breeding?

ERIC   I have. Since the cradle we have worked together, and I have his bread to be mine.

TIM   How fares he now?

ERIC   In the King's stables, my lord. Shall I send for him?

TIM   Stay you. And yet, are you not the office?

ERIC   I am as my lord will have me.

TIM   Then answer me this.

ERIC   I will try my lord, but I am not one such for answers .

TIM   Give your heart your mouth then and think not on it. Were the friend's need that of office thou wouldst be glad, would thee not.

ERIC   That in marriage they please you, aye, my lord.

TIM   And were they not?

ERIC   My lord?

TIM   Were they not one. Were friendship and duty in direct opposition, what have you then?

ERIC   Then I am office.

TIM   (VEXED) No! What are you? Not kith before crown?

SARAH (OFF) Are you down there.

TIM   (LOOKING OFF) Shit. Here comes the queen.

WILL STOPS TYPING AND THE CHARACTERS FREEZE. SARAH'S HEAD APPEARS THROUGH THE TRAP DOOR, ADDRESSING WILL.

SARAH   (SHARPLY) What are you doing up there.

WILL   (GUILTILY) Nothing.

SARAH PAUSES FOR A SECOND AND THEN RETREATS.

WILL LEANS FORWARD AND BEGINS TYPING AGAIN, HITTING THE DELETE KEY AND WIPING THE LAST LINE. THEN HE STARTS WRITING AGAIN IN EARNEST.

WILL   Enter Canterbury.

ENTER KEVIN FROM THE WINGS, DRESSED AS THE ARCHBISHOP OF CANTERBURY.

KEVIN   (BOTH VOICE AND ACTIONS ARE VERY DIFFERENT TO THE KEVIN WE SAW BEFORE, MORE CONFIDENT AND CONTROLLED) My king!

TIM   (HANDING THE TORCH BACK TO ERIC) Good Canterbury!

THE TWO MEN HUG.

TIM   Come you to me at this hour?

KEVIN   Hath the cock yet crowed?

TIM   Ne'er thrice. (THE TWO MEN LAUGH) The weather was with you?

KEVIN   Like God's hand itself, bearing me to thy service.

TIM   Ho! Blaspheme you still, holiness? (TO ERIC) Bring us mead. (TO KEVIN) You have not forsaken the grape?

KEVIN   Nor you, my lord.

EXIT ERIC .

TIM   Ah, but you have vexed me. And there's the truth of it.

KEVIN   Would that I could find some other way.

TIM   And what are the wits for if not the finding?

KEVIN   'Tis not finding you ask of me.

ENTER ERIC, A PITCHER OF MEAD IN EACH HAND.

TIM   What then?

KEVIN   Change.

TIM   Then change.

KEVIN   And would God? But look, mead and we are brothers.

THE TWO MEN TAKE THE DRINKS, EYEING EACH OTHER.

TIM   I am a son to you.

KEVIN   Older brother always, my king. And look at you. The very presence of England. Though France ever upon your arm.

TIM   As you like it.

KEVIN   A man to my knave!

TIM   How sits you with holiness?

KEVIN   Uneasy as always.

TIM   Yet at ease and at odds with me.

ENTER SARAH UNHEARD BY WILL. SHE CLIMBS THE LADDER AGAIN, NEITHER SEEING NOR HEARING THE CHARACTERS WHO EXIST ONLY IN WILL'S MIND. SHE WATCHES HIM TYPE.

KEVIN   Your courtiers, my lord. Not you.

TIM   And what am I if not the Crown?

KEVIN   And I but the robes.

TIM   I must have you with me on this!

KEVIN   How fares the Queen?

TIM   Fair that the morning thwarts her.

SARAH   It's a play isn't it?

WILL JUMPS AND STOPS TYPING. THE CHARAC-
TERS FREEZE. AND THEN MOVE OFF STAGE LEFT
TALKING SILENTLY AMONGST THEMSELVES IN
SOME DISAGREEMENT.

WILL   Jesus! You scared the shit out of me!

SARAH   You're writing another one of those plays, aren't
you?

WILL   It's just writing.

SARAH   There's no such thing as just writing. Not with
you.

WILL   I'm just writing!

SARAH   I thought we agreed you weren't going to write
plays anymore.

WILL   You agreed!

SARAH   Well, after you lost five thousand dollars I
thought one of us should! Did you go to the interview?

WILL   I went.

SARAH   And?

WILL   And I went! They don't offer jobs on the spot!

SARAH   Jesus!

WILL   It's just writing and anyway…

SARAH   You know, I got you that interview. I mean, that
cost me. You know? They're a good firm, and it cost me.
The least you could do is make a goddamned effort, you
know what I mean? Did you go like that?

WILL   I changed.

SARAH   Did you hang the suit back up?

WILL   (SHEEPISH) It's on the bed.

SARAH   Jesus!

WILL   Anyway, I might have picked up something.

SARAH   (SUSPICIOUS) What do you mean, picked up?

WILL   A directing job.

SARAH   You don't have any experience.

WILL   It's theatre. Shakespeare. They want me to take a pass at… At putting on one of his older plays. At revitalising it.

SARAH   And that's what you're doing now?

WILL   I'm… I'm editing it.

SARAH   What do you mean, editing?

WILL   I'm editing. It's like, three hours long and they need it cut down to two, and… and there's all the staging…

SARAH   Oh, Jesus. It's not another of those amateur church hall things again?

WILL   It's paid!

SARAH   Paid paid?

WILL   Paid paid.

SARAH   Where?

WILL   (MUMBLES) At the Lyceum.

SARAH   Where?

WILL   The Lyceum.

SARAH   That place from the thing?

WILL   It's…

SARAH   Oh, no. No! I'm going to phone Daddy and see if he can't speak to someone in the firm.

WILL   No!

SARAH   They said it was a lock . I want to know what went wrong.

WILL   Nothing went wrong.

SARAH   We'll see. (SHE STARTS TO DESCEND) And you better not spill any of that coffee up here. That comes through the ceiling and… (HER LAST WORDS ARE LOST AS SHE EXITS)

WILL MAKES A RUDE GESTURE.

WILL   (SOTTO) You fucking vampire blood-sucking witch!

SARAH (OFF, SHOUTING) You say something?

WILL   (LOUDLY) Nothing.

HE GOES TO THE EDGE, PEERS DOWN, AND THEN RETURNS TO HIS COMPUTER.

WILL (CONT.)   Act three, scene seven. The bitch dies. Enter Henry. Enter Placename. Enter knight.

THE PLAYERS MOVE BACK TO THE CENTRE WITH TIM AS THE KING, ERIC AS THE SERF, BUT KEVIN NOW DRESSED AS A KNIGHT.

TIM   His blood! His blood is on me!

ERIC   I see nothing, my lord.

TIM   (TURNING TO HIM) 'Tis here. 'Tis holy and devout, but it is audible to daylight. Ne'er shall I look to them again without the sight of it.

KEVIN   My lord. I do not understand. It was most prudent a manner.

TIM   Most prudent? To damn my own soul, and aye, thine with me!

KEVIN   My lord, your words!

TIM   Were words no more to action than thought is to deed!

KEVIN   My lord, I heard you clear as I stand now.

TIM PULLS A KNIFE AND RUSHES AT HIM, HOLDING IT UP TO HIS THROAT.

TIM   Then come hither and hear it!

ERIC   My lord!

TIM   I gave none but my word. My word none but my anger, and my office no order. Say you so?

KEVIN   But the queen bid us heed your words.

TIM   What say you?

KEVIN   My lord. The queen said, yesternight, that we four were to bear to your words as though parchment containing the royal seal.

ERIC   'Twas so, my lord. She said it thus.

TIM   (SAGGING) In a cathedral. Before God and

mammon. His blood cries out!

KEVIN   My lord, we made him bade peace and timely.

TIM   Good Thomas. You have cut off my hands.

ERIC   Yet hold they a knife.

TIM MOVES AWAY.

TIM   Wife! (QUIETER) My hands. (SHOUTING) Wife! Bide me now!

ENTER SARAH DRESSED AS THE QUEEN.

SARAH   My liege?

TIM   (TO KEVIN & ERIC) Get thee from my sight!

SARAH   What have you, sire? Is't the dead you wish to raise with your voice?

EXIT KEVIN .

TIM   'Twas my voice that sent them there!

THE TWO START TO CIRCLE EACH OTHER.

SARAH   My lord. Why starest thou at thy hands? Dost thou find the servants errant in their duty? I shall have them whipped.

TIM   Marbled queen! Do not seek to soften thy blows with pretence but let instead thy nature continue to rain down upon us!

SARAH   Why, you are mad. Or the like of it. I'll send for the physician.

TIM   Mad, aye. Yet not grief as would befit my countenance. In shame am I. In shame!

SARAH   Truly mad. We'll leech you!

TIM   I am a horse.

SARAH   Thou art a king and would act like one!

TIM   Then I am a cloud. Carried merry in the mournful sky.

SARAH   A king I say. Stop fucking around and stand up straight!

TIM   Why. A river then. Carry, carry.

SARAH   Why talk you thus?

TIM   Mark you not my words?

SARAH   When they are twinged and sagging? I do not.

TIM RALLIES ON HER AS IF TO STRIKE.

TIM   And yet this day, this very night you callest my knights so! Heed his words! Were I Adam that I could pluck my bone from your chest and free all men from the turpitude of womanhood.

SARAH (OFF, HER VOICE DRIFTING UP INTO THE ROOM, STOPPING THE CHARACTERS DEAD AS WILL PAUSES HIS TYPING TO LISTEN) Daddy says he's going to call the firm.

WILL (SHOUTING) Wonderful. (SOTTO) Bitch.

WILL RETURNS TO WRITING, TAPPING FURIOUS-LY AWAY.

TIM   Dog's daughter. I should have shied from your face ere it caught my eye!

SARAH   So, my king? And I still see you in all your glory.

TIM   This was in your eye!

SARAH   'Tis my luck and love to have all things you in it.

TIM   Thomas is dead!

SARAH   Then he is dead. Let angels weep for him. For us, we are about the living!

TIM   There is no living thing in you! Or none that thou woulds't not kill!

SARAH   Such is our circumspect!

SARAH (OFF, BUT THIS TIME WILL KEEPS TYPING AND THE CHARACTERS KEEP MOVING) Did you hear me?

WILL   I heard you!

TIM   It is not bones that can batter me thus!

SARAH (OFF) He's pretty angry about it. Says he had to pull a lot of strings just to get you in there!

SARAH And what is it that I hit? I married a man and made him king. I married dust and turned him into the world. God has not the shackles on me!

SARAH (OFF) Did you hear what I said?!

WILL (SHOUTING) I heard you!

TIM Wench you were and wench I will have you. Thomas is dead!

SARAH And the church is yours and with it, England's world! There's none now between you and God.

TIM Save the Pope!

SARAH (SMILING) Save the Pope.

WILL SITS BACK, TIRED. THE CHARACTERS FREEZE AS HE SCANS THE PAGE, THEN MOVE AS HE STARTS TYPING AGAIN.

TIM Sweet Eleanor. You have killed us.

SARAH Then I will raise us once more.

TIM Was it you?

SARAH Ever us.

TIM You that lit the stars. Drew the moon and guided man to gaze up at it.

SARAH That… might have been you.

TIM Your hand is in this!

SARAH My hand is in yours!

TIM Aye. I feel the grip of steel in it and how it twist-eth towards me.

SARAH (OFF) They want us to go round.

TIM I'm sure they do the fucking parasites.

WILL LEANS BACK AGAIN. THE CHARACTERS FREEZE

WILL What time?

SARAH (OFF) Eight.

WILL I can't tonight!

SARAH (OFF) They're cooking. I said we would so we're going.

WILL   (WHINING) I'm in the middle of something here!

SARAH (OFF) It's the least we can do seeing as they're helping us keep the roof over our heads!

WILL   (SOTTO) Jesus!

WILL LEANS FORWARD AND TYPES FAST AGAIN, ONCE MORE ANIMATING THE CHARACTERS.

TIM   What is it in man that makes him seek out his destruction in hair, in breath, in formliness?

SARAH   What in man that he be so contemptibly weak!?

TIM   Ah, you are a magnificent snake. Had I not lost one sibling enough for your liking?

SARAH   He was no blood.

TIM   He was flesh to my heart! Meat to my bones!

SARAH   You were weak with him.

TIM   I was tender!

SARAH   And what is that to a king?

SARAH (OFF) Come down and get changed.

TIM   For fuck's sake woman! I'm trying to write!

SARAH Look at you. You're pathetic!

SARAH (OFF) Did you hear me.

WILL / TIM   I heard you.

TIM   I hear nothing else. Nothing! Does't it not occur to your sweet nature that I am what your eye sees?

SARAH   Which is why you should take the job.

TIM   I dost not like it.

SARAH (OFF) Are you coming?

TIM   'Tis not for me.

WILL   In a minute!

SARAH   What is man if not the office that befits him? What husband if not a pay check?

TIM   Am I not king?

SARAH   I am Eleanor! Queen of France! Divorced and married at two score years. Queen of these green fields within but a half score.

TIM   I don't want to work in a goddamned bank!

SARAH 'Tis what we are.

TIM   Could you not leave me but him?!

SARAH He was your weakness.

TIM   I will fight you!

SARAH You have not the will. And I, I have your sons!

SARAH (OFF) William!

WILL & TIM In a minute!

SARAH (OFF) Not in a minute. Now!

WILL Alright. Alright!

TIM   What gods wished upon us woman? (HE MOVES CENTRE STAGE) What judges us of blood? Naught but a lack of pessary separate kith from kin. If the moon, in its heavenly splendour, choose none but the sun to guide him. If the seas find not turning unless upon his very edict, and man no more control them than he doth his nature, then I offer you this…

SARAH (OFF) We're going to be late!

WILL (YELLING) In a minute!

TIM   (GENTLY) … Let honour, goodness, and loyalty mark us. Let us not be equestrian in our nature, but bide us to what the mind hath set, the heart accepts, and temperance allows. I, for me, will have no more blood in my mind. The queen is gone. This very day will see her banished from our sight. An arc no more to be pleasured. Aye, and our sons with her and good. For I will have me a field. An acre of likeminded people, balanced, not on blood but on law and civility. For if blood knows only of itself, and hateth that which comest to it not. Then we will have water. In this land. On this day. We will have water and wash us clean of good Thomas.

SARAH (OFF, SHOUTING) If you're not down here in five minutes I'm going without you!

ENTER KEVIN AND ERIC, THIS TIME DRESSED AS
GUARDS.

TIM   The Queen's for the tower, (ADDING) and if you
want to rough her up a bit on the way there. Feel free.

KEVIN AND BOB TAKE THE QUEEN BY EACH
ARM.

CURTAIN.

END OF ACT II.

ACT III

The Dress Rehearsal

WE SEE THE STAGE OF THE LYCEUM, DECORAT-
ED AS A CASTLE HALL. ON THE STAGE IN PERIOD
COSTUME STAND KEVIN AS HENRY, TIM AS THE
BISHOP, ERIC AS HIS SERF, AND SAM AS ELEANOR.
ALL THREE HAVE SCRIPTS IN HAND, PRACTICING
THEIR LINES WORDLESSLY AT THE FIRST DRESS
REHEARSAL.
WILL SITS IN ONE OF TWO EMPTY SEATS UP-
STAIRS, DIRECTING.
KEVIN   Red lorry. Yellow lorry. Red lorry. Yellow lorry.
WILL   Alright. Not bad. I want to pick it up again from
the top of act two. We're getting there, but we're still miss-
ing that… oomph. Kevin, I still think we're not getting
enough out of you in terms of, you know, sexiness.
KEVIN   Never been much of one for that, true.
WILL   You're king. There's not a woman out there doesn't
want you.
KEVIN   Ah. The Stanislavski System!
WILL   Exactly. Let's pick it up from the top of page sixty,
yeah. And Sam. We're looking for a queen here, alright?
(THE CHARACTERS MOVE INTO POSITION. SAM
OFF TO THE SIDE . TIM IN THE WING) Eric. Bit be-
fore you come in, so you want to do Tim's lines for him?
ERIC   Thanks.
WILL (CONT.)   And… Enter Becket.
TIM WALKS ON STAGE AND BOWS DEEPLY. OVER-

ACTING, HIS MOVEMENTS ARE STAGED AND
COMICAL.

BEHIND, ERIC READS THE LINES BLANDLY AND
WITHOUT FEELING, STUMBLING OVER SOME OF
THE WORDS, DOING THE VOICE OF BECKET FOR
TIM WHO MIMES OUT THE MEANINGS.

ERIC   My lord!

KEVIN   Nay lord! Never king! Too dear is thy face to us
to be weighed with such solemnity.

ERIC   (AS THE TWO EMBRACE) Still king and ever
lord, for where there is title to the man there is man to
the title.

KEVIN   Speak you well, as ever you did. What brings
you to Canterbury?

ERIC   Come I hither for the sport, my lord.

KEVIN   The sport?

ERIC   Aye. Of playing jester to your crown.

KEVIN   'Tis never thus! Never. Still, sent for you I did,
and with weight and purpose I am vouch to say.

ERIC   You would have me Archbishop.

KEVIN   Ah, but you know my mind. Nay, the whole
of me you know, I grant, from britches to… (OUT OF
CHARACTER) …bugger.

SAM   Broadstrap.

WILL   Kevin!

KEVIN   From britches to broadstrap!

ERIC   Not in a hundred lifetimes, my lord. And were
you to live that long I'd like as much not answer what my
heart gives me. Heaven and all others know that I am not
the man you want for this burden.

KEVIN   Burden, is it? Burden! To be the most powerful
man in the kingdom, subject only to thy royal majesty?

ERIC   As ever I am. But there lies the rub.

KEVIN   (BREAKING CHARACTER) I still think that's

too much foreshadowing, you know? Someone's bound to notice.

SAM   Notice what?

KEVIN   Right. (BACK IN CHARACTER) What speak you man. Are you justice?

ERIC   As a scale I'd have you, my lord.

KEVIN   And temperate. I'll answer to that.

ERIC   My lord.

KEVIN   Yet you will not this for me? For what needs in a man but the qualities thou hath already professed to.

ERIC   Why, faith, my lord. Faith in heaven's answer.

KEVIN   And have you none?

ERIC   'Tis not mine own faith that is want, 'tis mother church. Rome!

KEVIN   But that is why you! See you not? Your faith is the heart of justice. The peace of it!

ERIC   Yet 'tis not the church's. 'Tis faith in faith itself for faith's sake.

KEVIN   Speak you plainly! Answer me. Is a priest not a man?

ERIC   He is so, my lord.

KEVIN   Doth he not eat?

ERIC   He does.

KEVIN   Doth he not think?

ERIC   At times, I grant you.

KEVIN   Cut, will he not cry?

ERIC   I have seen it so.

KEVIN   Then he is a man!

ERIC   The very countenance of it but…

KEVIN   But me no buts! (OUT OF CHARACTER) Too much?

ERIC   Yeah. Figure they'll know that one.

SAM   Thought that was Jesus.

THEY ALL LOOK AT HER, THEN MOVE BACK INTO

CHARACTER.

KEVIN   But me no buts! If priest is man he should act as one, be taxed as one, and fall under law as one. Speak, I beg you, for I think I am to have you on this!

ERIC   My lord…

KEVIN   (ANGRY) I will have you and have you mine, or you are no friend.

ERIC   But the deepest friend. A friend who sees his path leading away and plants a signpost.

KEVIN   Enough. You will! (SOFTENING) That you worry so becomes you, but I have your love. I know your justice. And know I to lean upon them.

ERIC   (ACQUIESCING) My lord.

KEVIN   Thank me not. 'Twas our lady queen who gave portent to the notion.

ERIC   Did she so?

KEVIN   Here comes she!

ERIC   My lady.

SAM MOVES INTO FRAY, PULLING HERSELF UPRIGHT INTO A QUEENLY POSE.

SAM   (AS ELEANOR) Why comest thou hither, my lord? Has my king sent for you?

ERIC   In so that it pleases your majesties.

KEVIN   'Twas your bidding.

ERIC   He has been charging me to reject my sins.

SAM   Would it were so, but my king loves your sins more than your saintliness I fancy.

KEVIN   Love I all the man!

ERIC   Your graces are too kind.

SAM   Have you made an offer of him?

KEVIN   I have made bent the bough, but he has yet to break under my yoke.

ERIC   Would that I could see my way.

SAM   Then mayhaps I might prevail upon him.

ERIC   I would that you could, my lady. But where a king moves that ne'er his wife treadeth afore is indeed rare.

SAM   Then listen you this. What is friend?

ERIC   That wilt do good.

SAM   And what remembrance should a king one who would not help him in his kingliness? Should he not call him traitor? Unworthy. Enemy?

ERIC   If it was good that friend did not, then enemy indeed.

KEVIN   Indeed!

ERIC   I am boxed as much as Christmas past.

KEVIN   Then yield man! I will have of thee friendship, and we will have of us a kingdom more just, temperate and yea, heavenly, that angels will minister to us from the garden.

ERIC   It is too much. Yield I on this, and mark me. Friend am I. Advisor I am. But archbishop must I be in breeding as much as in title. For no more couldst thou not be king once crown adorn thy framed head.

KEVIN   I will have it.

SAM   Aye, and I also. (ASIDE) For you are in my needle now.

ERIC   Would thou bid me stay?

KEVIN   Woulds't thou go?

ERIC   If your office I am to take there are prayers before both God and man must be made.

KEVIN   Then go. The office will be made true by day-light. Prepare thou my friend, body and soul, for I mean to shape this land as has never been done. Rome or no Rome. Charlemagne hath not seen the like of us yet.

ERIC   (BOWING LOW) My lady.

TIM MOVES BACK AND AWAY OUT OF THE SCENE.

KEVIN   Well have you, my Queen.

SAM   My lord.

KEVIN   I fare we make a good team, do we not?

SAM   I am your servant.

KEVIN   Now. None of that. You are my woman, my bed, and my mind as well.

SAM   If you will have me.

KEVIN   Aye. And that. What a queen you are! Devise you, had he some point in his making?

SAM   'Twas meekness that led him thus.

KEVIN   Aye. For he is meek. Well, there you have him, for vanity was not borne in that face but twas appropriated.

ENTER BOB FROM THE BACK, COMING DOWN THE AISLE.

BOB   How's it going?

SAM   Turn you to me.

WILL   Not bad.

KEVIN   What have you?

BOB   They're still using scripts?

SAM   Naught that isn't you.

KEVIN   Just to iron things out.

BOB   We open in two weeks!

KEVIN   My god, you're a queen. We must have sons. And sons a-plenty for if thy head, be it pretty in thought as well as vision, sat upon my shoulders the world would not stand against it.

SAM   Would they stand now?

KEVIN   Mayhaps. For we are still two hearts divided betwixt us.

SAM MOVES CLOSER TO TIM CAUGHT UP IN THE ACTING, KISSING CLOSE.

SAM   And what distance have they now?

KEVIN   None for the finding.

SAM   Then in science none, in matrimony none, what is

there?

KEVIN   My god, you are a queen. My eyes have it in me to kiss you!

SAM   (BREAKING CHARACTER) Alright.

THE TWO GO IN KISSING CLOSE.

WILL   Annnd…..Cut!

BOB   That better have been acting.

WILL   (TO BOB) It was. (TO ALL) Okay. Once more from the top again, please! (TO BOB) Least, I think it was.

SAM   (TO ALL) Can we get him to like, floss or something? (TO KEVIN) Can you floss?

WILL   Kevin?

KEVIN   My teeth are mine own thanks to alcohol, I'll have you know.

BOB   (TO WILL) You're pretty up.

KEVIN   Kills the germs.

WILL   Alright, alright. Time's against us so from the top, if you please!

SAM   I thought the smell was germs!

WILL   (TO BOB) It's going well. (TO ALL) Eric. Take five alright? I want Tim without the words this time.

ERIC NODS AND HEADS OFF. THE REST MOVE BACK INTO THEIR ORIGINAL POSITIONS.

EXIT ERIC.

TIM ENTERS AND BOWS.

KEVIN   Nay lord! Never king! Too dear is thy face to us to be weighed with such solemnity.

THE TWO EMBRACE.

KEVIN   Speak you well, as ever you did. What brings you to Canterbury?

TIM STRIKES A SPORTING POSTURE.

KEVIN   The sport?

TIM MIMES A JESTER.

KEVIN   'Tis never thus! Never. Still, sent for you I did, and with weight and purpose I am vouch to say.

BOB   (STANDING UP AND WALKING DOWN TOWARDS THE STAGE) No, no! Stop! (THE ACTORS TURN TO LOOK AT HIM) (TO WILL) He gonna do that all the time.

WILL   It was that or a hidden speaker.

BOB   What… Look…. (HE TURNS TO TIM) Listen, I'm sorry, son. You're a great actor, you know, but Christ! (HE TURNS TO WILL WHO IS COMING DOWN THE AISLE AFTER HIM, A PIECE OF PAPER IN HIS HAND.) Shakespeare has words! Words! I mean, that's what Shakespeare is fucking about! Old words!

ENTER ERIC, A CUP OF TEA IN HIS HAND.

WILL   It's alright.

BOB   Look, I mean, hell, you're the writer and everything but I think they're going to notice that the fucking character doesn't speak, you know? They're going to fucking know, you know? It's not Shakespeare!

WILL   You knew he was mute!

BOB   Yeah, but I thought he was going to be a fucking extra or something. In the background. Not just, you know, miss lines!

KEVIN   If I could intrude.

BOB   No, you cannot fucking intrude and that better not be fucking real wine in that glass or you're out of here! (TO WILL) The script you gave me had lines! There were no fucking mutes!

ERIC   (OFFENDED FOR TIM) Hey!

BOB   There are no mutes in Shakespeare!

WILL   Calm down.

BOB   Calm down! We're two weeks from opening and you've got a fucking mute in the lead, they don't know their lines, and (POINTING TO KEVIN) he's drunk.

KEVIN   I may be drunk, sir, but…

BOB   Stow it. You're no Churchill.

KEVIN   I do a wonderful Churchill.

BOB   You do a wonderful lush.

ERIC   Tea, anyone? (HE IS IGNORED)

KEVIN   I'll have you know that I do all my shows drunk. 'Tis the only way to truly act!

BOB   Jesus. That's it. I'm pulling the show.

WILL   Wait. Wait! Look. Calm down. Everything's fine.

BOB TAKES THE PAPER PROFFERED TO HIM AND LOOKS AT IT.

BOB   What's this?

WILL   It's the copy for the program. I sent it off to the printer this morning.

BOB   (LOOKING HARD AT WILL BEFORE STARTING TO READ) "Live Door Productions Presents…" I like that. Live Door. Good sound to it.

WILL   Skip down.

BOB   "William Shakespeare's Henry the Second by Troubled Act Theatre Group."

SAM   I thought of that.

BOB   (NOT CARING) It's wonderful. "The script, revised and directed by Will Burrows especially for this production, blends modern artistry with classic stereotypes to produce a thoughtful, humorous, and, above all, challenging representation of the classic play." So?

WILL   (POINTING AT THE PAPER) Down here.

BOB   What's this?

WILL   The director's notes. Second paragraph.

BOB   (READING) "It seemed to me, while reading the play, that the role of Becket, while central, was superfluous to the battle of the sexes being waged in the classic text between Henry and Eleanor, and while most previous interpretations of the text have emphasized Becket's death scene, especially his soliloquy in act four," - goes on a bit, doesn't it? – "the character is nothing but a meta-phor for the death of the relationship between the great king and his wife." Alright. I like the classic text bit, but…

WILL   Next line.

BOB   (RELUCTANT TO CONTINUE) "Once this was determined, the decision to remove all lines from the part of Becket, rendering him mute, a shadow and foil for this gender struggle, was a relatively easy one." You gotta be fucking me!

WILL   He can do it! You saw him down there. It's per-fect!

BOB   You can't just cut a character's lines!

WILL   Why not. Most modern interpretations of Ham-let have cut his father's lines. It makes him more ghostly. And he can do it! Really. This is what the critics want. This is what they'll write about! This is the hook. Any-one can do Shakespeare. People want… more. This is the hook!

BOB   (TO SAM) Honey?

SAM   I think it works.

BOB   Yeah?

WILL   No one's ever cut a central character in Shake-speare before.

BOB   But this ain't Shakespeare!

WILL   They don't know that! No one does. Far as they're concerned we just cut the central character. The New Yorker alone will do an entire page on it. Good or bad.

(BOB REMAINS UNCONVINCED)

KEVIN   It is the nature of the stage.

ERIC   He's right.

KEVIN   It is art, not artifice. One cannot simply… bring it. One has to…

ERIC   Brung it?

SAM   (COMING OVER TO BOB) Sweetheart, it's actually quite good…

BOB   (CAVING) Yeah? (TO WILL) Alright. You're the artistic one. (TO THE CAST) Take five or something alright. Will and I got to talk.

THE CAST WALK UPSTAGE. BOB AND WILL MOVE DOWNSTAGE.

WILL   You alright? You seem uptight.

BOB   It's just got to be good, that's all. I don't want any half-assed…

WILL   It's good, boss. Really. I'm actually surprised at how good it is.

BOB   About seating.

WILL   Shoot.

BOB   We got about a hundred print media showing up opening night.

WILL   Jesus! Really? It's just Shakespeare! Who even reviews Shakespeare anymore?

BOB   Yeah, well. I know a man who knows everyone. Not going to be a problem?

WILL   Umm. Hell. No. But listen, keep it to yourself. alright? I don't want them panicked.

BOB   That's what I thought. Thing is, media don't make no noise. We got to fill the rest of the seats, you know? Give them an ambience.

WILL   Shouldn't be a problem.

BOB   But we can't have any luvvies either. No one that's going to know that this isn't Shakespeare. None of your lot. You catch my drift? Don't want them tipping the wink in the interval. Know what I mean?

WILL   Good point.

BOB   We're going to need regular on-the-street people. I was thinking of just giving out tickets to the people in my offices but, hell, they have to actually like Shakespeare otherwise they're just going to go to sleep.

WILL   Yeah.

BOB   So what we need are educated, intelligent people who don't know their ass from their elbow. Got another hundred covered with onlookers but… Got any ideas?

WILL   Students?

BOB   Brilliant! Think they know everything, and wouldn't admit to it if they didn't. Wonderful!

KEVIN (CALLING OVER) Author!

WILL   Yo.

KEVIN   So sorry to interrupt you good sires, but they request we vacate so they can clean. We did say till four.

WILL   (LOOKING AT HIS WATCH) Yeah, alright. (LOUDLY) Everyone! We'll meet back at seven backstage for a reading. And no notes this time! I want it memorized, okay?

ALL   Sure / Fine (etc)

THE CAST EXIT LEAVING WILL AND BOB ALONE ON THE STAGE. THE LIGHTS CLICK OFF, CASTING THEM INTO DIMNESS.

EXIT KEVIN, SAM, ERIC, TIM.

BOB PULLS OUT HIS MOBILE PHONE.

BOB   Let's get lunch.

WILL   Great. Listen, I know a few people at the university. Want me to spread the word?

BOB   (DIALLING) No need. I own a wing.

WILL   No professors though!

BOB   Think they'd know?

WILL   Doubt it. Just don't want them criticizing my edit.

THE LIGHTS CUT OUT, CASTING THE STAGE INTO BLACKNESS.

BOB   Hello? Goddamned reception's out.

THERE'S A LOUD BANG.

WILL   Shit!

BOB   What?

WILL   Fell off the stage.

BOB   Yeah? Well. Break a leg. Come on.

THE PAIR HEAD UP THE AISLE TOWARDS THE DOOR .

WILL   Do you mind if I ask you how you met?

BOB   Who?

WILL   Sam. Samantha.

BOB   Son, there are only two things in the world you never let people see how you make. One is money. The other is marriage.

WILL   And sausages.

BOB   Nah. Sausages are a metaphor. You need to see how that's done.

EXIT BOB AND WILL.

END OF ACT III.

ACT IV

The Party

THERE IS A SOUND OF DISTANT APPLAUSE.
CURTAINS.
WE OPEN ON THE TRAP DOOR, AS IN ACT ONE,
ONLY THIS TIME IT'S EMPTY. THE SOUND OF AP-
PLAUSE GROWS LOUDER AND THE DOOR TO THE
BAR OPENS.
ENTER WILL, BOB, SAM, ERIC, KEVIN, AND TIM.
KEVIN, SAM AND TIM ARE DRESSED IN COS-
TUMES AS BEFORE. WILL AND BOB ARE IN TUXE-
DOS.
IT'S THE SECOND NIGHT OF THE PLAY AND IT'S
ANOTHER FULL HOUSE, THE FIRST WHERE PEO-
PLE HAVE BOUGHT TICKETS.

KEVIN   Drinks!

BOB   Champagne!

WILL   I can't believe it. Where'd all those people come from?

ERIC   (PULLING A COUPLE OF CHAMPAGNE BOT-
TLES FROM BEHIND THE BAR) Sally, she works in box office, she said they were phoning all day.

BOB   There was a queue. (TO ERIC) Lock the door.

SAM   Did you hear that curtain call? They loved us!

ERIC   Think we might have to stay open.

WILL   They loved you! You were great!

BOB   Private party.

ERIC   Last night was a private party.

BOB   Tonight's the private-private party. Lock the door.

ERIC GOES AND LOCKS THE DOOR.

WILL   What's going on?

BOB   Nothing. We're celebrating. God, I can't believe a play can actually make money. You know?! I mean. Fuck! If I'd known all it took to make money was a few words and a stage I wouldn't have bought into Facebook.

WILL   (TO ERIC) Hey, what about the stagehands? Extras?

BOB   Fuck 'em. They had last night. Tonight it's just the six of us.

WILL   What's going on?

BOB   (HOLDING UP A CHAMPAGNE BOTTLE) To you guys. You were great up there tonight. (TO SAM) Sweetheart, god, I was so proud of you. You looked fantastic. Kevin, man – I take it all back. I thought you couldn't pull it off, you know? But you were the balls, really. (EVERYONE LAUGHS) Eric. You were on the money my friend.

WILL   You were the glue!

BOB   Really. (TO TIM) Tim. What can I say? Can this boy act or can this boy act? We cut off another of your extremities and you'll be up for an Oscar, no kidding. And Will. You did it, son. All of you. You're a success. How does it feel?

BOB POPS A CORK. WILL DOES LIKEWISE AND EVERYONE CHEERS. IGNORING GLASSES THEY PASS THE BOTTLES. EVERYONE IS DRINKING, KEVIN TOO LONG AND WILL TAKES IT BACK OFF HIM. BOB CLIMBS UP ONTO A TABLE, FACING THEM.

BOB   Alright. Alright! And now the moment you've all been waiting for! Will didn't want you to read them before tonight, but now that it's done. (HE HOLDS UP THE PAPERS) Reviews!

THERE'S COLLECTIVE GROANING.

BOB (CONT.) Yeah, yeah. Look, I think you can tell from tonight that last night was a success. But the question I know you're all asking is… Did anyone find out? (HE OPENS UP THE PAPERS) Let's see.

KEVIN   My friends, my ears cannot heed the sound of negativity without at least a quart of bourbon…

ERIC   Bottle's behind the counter.

KEVIN   Cheers.

KEVIN MOVES BEHIND THE BAR AND STARTS POURING HIMSELF A DRINK. WILL AND TIM ALSO PULL OUT GLASSES AS BOB BEGINS TO READ.

BOB   Okay. This is the Times first. "Never before has a play so poor in origin been turned around so artfully as the Lyceum's Henry the Second…" (A CHEER GOES UP) "Not only is this play one of Shakespeare's least performed, it is one that most critics agree to be his worst."

ERIC   My god. They know nothing!

BOB   (READING ON) "Kudos should be given to the emerging talent of first-time director William Burrows' – that's you – 'for editing that goes so far as to completely restructure the play, providing light and life where there was only darkness and hegemony."

WILL   What the hell is he talking about?

BOB   There's more. "But high praise must go to the cast, who…" – sorry Will – "…turn what is at best mediocre wording…"

ERIC   What does he know!

BOB   "…into a tour de force of acting, particularly Ms. Samantha Millar…" – honey! – "…wife of…" – yadda yadda yadda – "…who lights up the stage with her anger and beauty, and Mister Timothy Westin, an unknown in a key role, who portrays more with a lack of words than Shakespeare did with the entire play."

THE GROUP APPLAUD AND PAT TIM ON THE BACK. BOB HOLDS UP ANOTHER PAPER.

BOB (CONT.) The Herald. "Henry the Great." (ANOTHER) The Star. "As we like it." (ANOTHER) The Globe. "Paint drying." (THE GROUP IS SILENT. BOB SMILES) They may hate it. But they still think it's Shakespeare!

WILL   Hell, a snub from the Globe is a virtual encore. They haven't loved anything since Spiderman!

BOB   Unanimous, then. You're great! You did it. Will, not only do they think it's Shakespeare, they love the edit. I didn't give that dumb thing a go, but you knew it! You knew it and you were right!

WILL   Salute!

BOB JUMPS DOWN FROM THE TABLE AND THROWS THE PAPERS TOWARDS THE GROUP WHO PICK THEM UP EAGERLY AND START TO READ.

BOB   Enjoy. There'll be more tomorrow.

SAM COMES OVER TO HIM.

SAM   Was I beautiful?

BOB   Are you ever not?

SAM   You're happy.

BOB   I won big tonight, baby. Bigger than you know. (THEY KISS) I got you.

SAM   Were you gonna lose me?

BOB   You can never tell.

(THEY KISS AGAIN, THEN BOB MOTIONS TO WILL)

BOB   Come here.

THE PAIR DRAW APART FROM THE GROUP WHO GO ON CELEBRATING.

WILL   Listen, in case I don't get another chance. Thank you.

BOB   What for?

WILL   For this!

BOB   (LAUGHS) Listen. I've been a success since I was a kid, you know? I mean, I haven't always won but, you know, let's just say I've won more than I lost, alright. But tonight. This? This was you, young man. All you. Now, I won't kid you and I'm not going to go into details either, but suffice it to say I did big tonight. Huge big. And you know, you did that. You!

WILL   Bob. I can honestly say I have no idea what you're talking about.

BOB   I've always betted. The whole thing, life. It's a gamble. I get this feeling that perhaps there's something better that we should be doing with our time but until someone tells me what it is, it's making money and I've always made money. Always have. But I've never betted on someone else before. It's a good feeling, you know? It feels good. I saw something in you. Something of me.

WILL   That means a lot.

BOB   Yeah, well. Not too much. Just… something. Only, (HE SEEMS TO BE ABOUT TO SAY SOMETHING, THEN DECIDES AGAINST IT) Doesn't matter. Listen, what I wanted to say is this. First, I've done what I needed to do with this play. I'll continue to finance it if it needs financing, but any money it makes is yours, ok?

WILL   (TAKEN ABACK) I don't know what to say.

BOB   Yeah, well. Split it with them, yeah.

WILL   I will.

ENTER SARAH THROUGH THE NOW UNLOCKED DOOR AND WALKS ACROSS THE ROOM UNNOTICED.

BOB   Second thing. Not sure how it'll go down yet, but

I'm thinking of buying this place. After tonight it's going to be something of a mecca for a certain type of people. Mine and yours, know what I mean? Whatever the case, I want you to write a play. A real play. Make it about whatever the hell you like. Shit, put a monkey throwing crap up on stage for three hours, no skin off my nose. Put it on and I'll fund it. Gratis.

WILL   That's… Thank you. Really.

BOB   You're a good kid, you know that.

WILL   Thank you.

BOB   Don't hug me or nothing.

WILL HUGS HIM. BOB HUGS BACK.

BOB   Your wife know you feel like that about men?

SARAH TAPS WILL ON THE SHOULDER, AND WHEN HE TURNS TO SEE HER SHE KISSES HIM PASSIONATELY, HER PREVIOUS ANIMOSITY LOST. WILL PULLS AWAY.

WILL   Mmmm. Hey. I thought you were upstairs.

SARAH   I wanted to be with you.

WILL   I was just…

SARAH   They love it! Even Daddy thinks it's good. I'm proud of you. (WILL LOOKS AWKWARD) What?

WILL   You're proud of me?

SARAH   Of course! It's a success.

WILL   And that's the measure of it, is it?

SARAH   What do you mean.

BOB   Your husband has outdone himself, Mrs. Burrows.

SARAH   It's… Thank you.

BOB   I've never been a writer but I know a couple, and there's one thing that marks a good writer from a bad one. A complete lack of perspective.

SARAH   You've… I'm sorry, you've read Will's work?

WILL   Ah.

BOB   Read? I saw it tonight. Heard it, rather.

SARAH   Mr. Williams. I'm sorry. Will didn't wr… You mean the edit?

BOB   (TO WILL) She doesn't know?

WILL No.

SARAH Know?

WILL I hadn't got round to telling her yet.

SARAH I'm sorry. I don't understand.

BOB   My dear lady. Your husband is the perpetrator of the biggest hoax on the New York public since Rudy Giuliani ran for mayor.

SARAH I'm… What?

BOB   Mrs. Burrows. Your husband wrote this play.

SARAH He wrote it?

WILL Sarah…

BOB   Every goddamed word. Well, not every word. He stole some lines from Marlowe but…

WILL Sarah.

SARAH Mr. Williams. I'm afraid you don't seem to understand. Are you saying that… (TURNING TO WILL) Will, what is he saying?

BOB   Your husband wrote the play.

SARAH Shakespeare!

BOB   No.

SARAH But I read it in school.

BOB   Hmm. Perhaps this is something the pair of you need to discuss privately.

WILL Sarah…

SARAH Mr. Williams. I'm sorry. I mean, don't get me wrong here. Will directed this. But it's a Shakespeare play.

ENTER LOVITZ.

BOB GOES OVER TO LOVITZ AS HE ENTERS, BLOCKING HIS WAY.

WILL I know. I wrote it!

BOB   Private party.

LOVITZ PULLS OUT A CARD AND HANDS IT TO BOB.

SARAH   On a level, sure…

BOB EXCUSES HIMSELF.

WILL   On paper!

BOB   Really?

LOVITZ NODS AND BOB WAVES HIM IN.

SARAH   It's a Shakespeare play!

WILL   (SOTTO) It's not. Really. I wrote it.

SARAH   I read it in school! I think I did a paper on it!

WILL   (CONSCIOUS OF THE NEW MAN IN THE ROOM, KEEPING HIS VOICE LOW) You didn't. I mean, it's a famous story so perhaps you did. Auden did a play on it, but it's not Shakespeare.

SARAH   Will, honey. You're a success. No one is doubting that. But it's Shakespeare!

LOVITZ INTERRUPTS.

LOVITZ   Excuse me. Looking for the director. Will Burrow?

WILL   Burrows. (LOOKING OVER AT BOB WHO SMILES) What can I do for you?

KEVIN COMES OVER, A CURIOUS LOOK ON HIS FACE.

LOVITZ   You're Burrows?

WILL   And you are?

KEVIN   Do I know you, sir?

LOVITZ   (HANDING A CARD TO WILL) Jim Lovitz. I do production work for Mandalay.

WILL   Movies?

LOVITZ   Well. We produce them. We're a production company. We don't actually film them or anything. We… green light them.

WILL   I see. What brings you to New York, Mr Lovitz?

LOVITZ   Can I get a drink, perhaps?

SARAH   Mr. Lovitz. I'm Sarah Burrows…

WILL   Sarah. Get Mr. Lovitz…

LOVITZ   Jim.

WILL   …Jim a drink. Okay?

SARAH   (TAKEN ABACK BY HIS FORCE) Huh.

WILL   A drink. Mr. Lovitz. Thank you.

LOVITZ   Really. It's Jim.

SARAH GOES TO GET HIM A DRINK.

KEVIN   We've met.

WILL   Did you like the show?

LOVITZ   Loved it. Loved it! Flew in specially from L.A. this evening!

WILL   Well, we're flattered.

SARAH RETURNS WITH THE DRINK AND HANDS IT WORDLESSLY TO LOVITZ.

LOVITZ   Yeah, no. I think there's a great project here.

WILL   Well, I don't know about that.

KEVIN   We're theatre people, Mr Lovitz. We don't do projects. We do plays!

WILL   My colleague is right. Tactless, but right I'm afraid.

LOVITZ   (PACING) That's too bad, you know.

WILL   We like what we do.

LOVITZ   I'm sure you do.

WILL   It's nothing personal. I'm sure your company makes excellent films.

LOVITZ   Nah. They're crap. Intellectual garbage designed for eighteen year olds with IQ's under a hundred. (SITTING DOWN, HE LOOKS AGAIN AT BOB) Hey, you're Robert Williams, aren't you?

WILL   As I was saying…

LOVITZ   (STANDING AGAIN) Sure, sure. I get it. Private party. Shame really.

ERIC   Why's that?

LOVITZ   It's just that I think I can get this green lit. That's all.

KEVIN   How proud you must be.

LOVITZ   See. I woke up this morning and google searched the papers. Much easier than reading them. And I came across the Times' thing on this little... Let's call it a production, shall we? And I thought to myself: this I gotta see. So I fly out here, then and there. Had a lunch meeting with Richard E Kelly but blew it right off. Hopped on a plane, got here before I left.

WILL   Like I said. We're flattered. Really. It's just that... Well...

LOVITZ   Sure, I get it. You're play people. You're not interested in a movie deal. Doesn't matter I suppose. We'll do it anyway.

KEVIN   What do you mean?

LOVITZ   Hey, Shakespeare's hot on the straight to video market at the moment. Figure we can get Branagh. I know we can get Pacino! I think it's got real screen potential!

SAM   You can't do that!

WILL   Samantha...

LOVITZ   Sure we can. Sure we can. Shakespeare's public property. Anyone can do Shakespeare! Shame really.

ERIC   Why's that?

LOVITZ   He was alive, hell, we'd give him six figures for it. Seven for the making rights. Play like this, rights would be even higher.

KEVIN   You can't do this.

LOVITZ   Really? Why's that?

SARAH   My husband wrote it.

WILL   (TURNING SHARPLY ON HER) No!

SARAH STARES AT HIM DUMBFOUNDED.

BOB   Alright. What do we all say we give them some room?

LOVITZ   See, here's what I think. You're in a bind. That's what I think!

BOB   That's enough!

LOVITZ   I was looking at the Times. Henry the Second. And I just started laughing, you know. Because, hell, everyone knows there ain't no Henry the Second. Not in Shakespeare.

KEVIN   As if you'd know the Bard!

LOVITZ   Sure I do. Sure I do! I went to high school! Only. No one here seems to get it, do they? They don't know. You've fooled the entire theatregoing public of New York, and that puts you in a bind!

ERIC   How so?

WILL   Because if I tell anyone, I'll never get an audience again.

LOVITZ   Bingo! New York's a theatre town. People you've conned. They don't like being conned! You'll never get a write up again! Not a good one, and you know that. That's why you haven't told anyone yet. Am I right?

BOB   Will?

WILL   They'll never come again. They'll think it's another hoax.

LOVITZ   So on the one hand you come clean. You come clean right and you've got the whole talk show scene, the whole fame thing, but no more theatre. And on the other, you've got a glorious career as the best man since Olivier.

SARAH   Honey?

BOB   I'll bankroll you.

WILL   It doesn't matter. No one will come. I'll be a joke.

LOVITZ   Or not. You let me out you. You let Mandalay do it. You get the movie rights, you get the talk show rights, and we'll give you a green light on whatever project you got next plus six figures.

ERIC   Shit.

LOVITZ   And you. (HE LOOKS AROUND) All of you get parts! (BEAT) Small parts.

KEVIN   Will?

LOVITZ   You see. Movie people. We're not like theatre people. We know what people want and we give it to them. And people, they want tits and ass, guns and ammo. And occasionally, to break the monotony of mindlessness, they want a little bit of Shakespeare. Not too much. Just once every three years. That kind of thing. You theatre people! You all think you're so great. So above us! And why? Because you don't make any decent money? Because you tailor to the intellectual effete? Because you have a character talking for longer than ten seconds at a time? But look at these people. Shit, they don't even know their Shakespeare! The only reason they know something is art is if someone tells them. And the people who tell them can't tell A Midsummer's Night's Dream from Deep Throat. (TO SAM) No offence.

SAM   None taken.

LOVITZ   So ask yourself this. You can't change it. Feed them Jessica Alba or feed them August Strindberg. They still all got to be fed. Question you got to ask yourself is this. Are you smart enough to make money doing it?

WILL TURNS TO THE GROUP.

WILL   Kevin?

KEVIN NODS.

WILL   Eric?

ERIC   It's what we're here for.

WILL   Thank you. Tim.

TIM NODS.

ERIC   You're sure.

TIM PAUSES, THEN HOLDS UP HIS HANDS IN SUR-

RENDER.

WILL   Sam?

SAM   What?

BOB   She's with you.

WILL   Ok. Bob. This okay with you?

BOB   Whatever you want, kid. Whatever you want.

WILL   Thank you.

SARAH   I'm proud of you, honey.

WILL   (IGNORING HER, HE EXTENDS A HAND TO LOVITZ) Thank you very much, Mr Lovitz. Enjoy your flight back to LA.

LOVITZ   You're sure?

WILL   We'd be grateful if you keep this conversation to yourself.

LOVITZ   Really?

WILL   Really.

LOVITZ   No problem. You change your mind…

BOB   We won't.

LOVITZ   Well. Okay then.

LOVITZ MOVES TO EXIT.

WILL   Oh, and Mr. Lovitz.

LOVITZ   Yes?

WILL   I like movies. I like people. I just don't like working for an industry that hates them both, that's all.

LOVITZ   Tell me that when you're writing dog food commercials, won't you.

EXIT LOVITZ.

SARAH   What did you just do?

WILL   Sarah…

SARAH (ANGRY) What did you just do?

BOB   Why don't we…

SARAH   Shut up! All of you. Just shut up! Millions, Will! He was offering you millions!

WILL   It's not about the money.

SARAH   Of course it's about the money! It's always about the money!

SAM   It's not, you know.

SARAH   He'll just make the movie without you!

WILL   He said it himself. He can't. People would know.

KEVIN   Of course, he could make a movie about faking a Shakespeare play.

WILL   Just not this one.

SARAH   Why the hell not!

WILL   It'd break intellectual copyright.

SARAH   Are you insane! Intellectual copyright? He was offering money, Will! Money! (SHE STARES AT WILL, DUMBFOUNDED, QUESTIONING WHO THIS MAN IS IN FRONT OF HER) I…

WILL   It's okay.

SARAH   I've got to go.

WILL   Yeah.

SARAH   I just gotta go, you know.

WILL   Yeah.

SARAH   I'll see you back at the…

SARAH STARES AT HIM FOR A MINUTE. THE GROUP WATCH AWKWARDLY IN SILENCE. THEN SHE TURNS TO GO.

SAM   Sometimes it's just about faith.

SARAH   Honey, faith is what you have when belief's left you.

WORDLESSLY SARAH GATHERS HER THINGS AND HEADS UP THE STAIRS WITHOUT LOOKING BACK.

EXIT SARAH.

THE GROUP BREATHE A COLLECTIVE SIGH OF RELIEF.

BOB   (TO WILL) Woman sure knows how to exit. I'll give her that.

WILL Yeah.

BOB She'll be alright. Once she thinks about it.

WILL (BREATHING OUT) No. No, she won't.

BOB Yeah. You're probably right. You know? There's only one thing you have to like.

WILL Writing?

BOB Yourself. It's the only constant you're ever gonna really have. That, and cirrhosis of the liver.

ERIC So we don't tell anyone?

WILL No one.

BOB You're not worried someone will notice?

WILL In the press? Sure. Eventually. But they can hardly say anything, can they?

BOB I'll see that they don't.

KEVIN (JUMPING UP) I have it.

WILL What?

KEVIN (STEPPING CENTRE STAGE AND GESTURING WILDLY) Curtain opens on a bar. Broken playwright sits centre stage.

ERIC Handsome barman stands behind the bar.

KEVIN Dashing actors surround!

THE GROUP STARTS WARMING TO IT. BOB AND WILL MOVE OFF CENTRE STAGE.

SAM Is there a part for me?

KEVIN My dear, heaven has a leading role worked out for you! I'm sure we can fit you in somewhere.

BOB (TO WILL) You alright, kid?

WILL You out of here?

BOB Market's open in New York.

WILL Money to make.

BOB I like to think of it in terms of people. Careers.

WILL Fortunes?

BOB (LOOKING AT HIS WATCH) Listen, you ever been to a club?

WILL   I'm not much for dancing.

BOB   Yeah, 'cos that's what we're dressed for. No. I've got this club a couple of blocks from here. Think you'll like it.

WILL   Now?

BOB   Why not?

WILL   What about them?

BOB   They'll be here.

THE TWO MOVE TOWARD THE EXIT .

ENTER FOOL.

BOB (CONT.) Anyway. Not sure they'd fit in.

WILL   And I do?

BOB LOOKS HIM UP AND DOWN.

BOB   Tonight you do. Yeah. Tomorrow who knows, right?

THE PAIR ARE AT THE EXIT AND WILL STOPS TO LOOK AROUND, THEN TURNS AND FOLLOWS BOB OUT OF THE DOOR.

FOOL Come friends, all things must have their ends
And this we know, no story bends
Away from where the fates decree
Not in love, or life, or poetry.
A love is lost, a purpose won,
A marriage proved; the play is done.
For the truth of all the stars is this:
No ending comes without amiss.
But until our mortal coil shrugs off
We face the crowd, we bow, we quaff.
And though no man here knows how he ends
We would hope in the presence of such friends.
But if we spirits have offended
Think but this and all is mended.
For, as I am an honest fool,
All stories bend to endings rule.

Else the Fool a liar call
So, good night unto you all.
Give me your hands, if we be friends,
The bar is open, the play: it ends.

CURTAINS.
END OF ACT IV.
THE END.

.

ORIGINAL PROGRAMME

The original production of Writing William contained an extra act and several characters which were eventually dropped from later productions due to time constraints.

Performed in Tokyo, the original programme contains translated synopsis of each of the five acts.

PROGRAM

ACT 1

Will, a playwright, leaves the production of his new play in the theatre above and spends the second act in the theatre bar, wondering how to tell his wife that the play is a flop. In the bar he meets an assortment of aging actors who try to comfort him, and a billionaire investor, Bob, who tries to convince him to write a fake Shakespeare play.

舞台では、劇作家ウィルの新しい芝居が上演されている。ウィルは席を立ち、この芝居が失敗作だったということをどう妻に話そうか考えながら、第2幕の間、階下のバーで時間を潰す。バーで彼はいろいろな老俳優たち、そして、億万長者の投資家、ボブと出会う。老俳優たちはウィルを慰め、ボブはシェークスピア作と偽って芝居を書けとウィルを説得する。

ACT 2

At home again, and in his office, Will, returning from a failed interview in a bank, tries to write scenes from the play, while having a fight with his wife.

ウィルは銀行の面接を受けるがうまくいかない。帰宅し、書斎で妻とけんかしながら芝居の場面を書こうとする。

30mins	INTERMISSION
30 分	休憩

ACT 3

At a prestigious club, Bob tells his peers of the upcoming play and proposes an audacious bet. One which could make him very rich indeed, or return his wife to working as a hostess.

一流クラブで、ボブはクラブのメンバーたちに近く上演される芝居のことを話し、そして無謀な賭けを提案する。本物の大富豪になるか、はたまた、再び妻をホステスとして働かせることになるかの賭け。

ACT 4

At rehearsals, Bob explains some of the plan to Will and worries about the performance.

リハーサルで、ボブは計画の一部をウィルに説明し、上演の心配をする。

5mins	INTERMISSION
5 分	休憩

ACT 5

The play a success, the cast gather in the bar to read reviews. Confronted by both his wife and a highly profitable proposition, Will finds himself with a choice to make.

芝居は成功。役者たちは批評を読みにバーに集まる。ウィルの前には妻と大きな儲け話が立ちはだかり、彼は選択を迫られる。

Henry II

Will Burrows makes a wise choice of subject for his counterfeit Shakespeare play, for indeed it is quite surprising that none of the great Elizabethan and Jacobean dramatists should have picked up on the story of Henri D'Anjou, who became Henry II, King of England. Perhaps Christopher Marlowe would have been the best man to dramatise the events of a life that included serial adultery, homosexuality, murder and incessant revolts, intrigues, the murder of his best friend and the imprisonment of his wife.

Lambeth Palace Library, London
The murder of Thomas Becket from a 15th century manuscript

As well as being the head of one of history's most dysfunctional families, Henry is perhaps best remembered for his quarrel with his Archbishop of Canterbury, Thomas A'Beckett. At the time Europe was riven by the struggle between the church and the secular rulers over dominance of the land, it's people and the money that went with it.

Thomas had been one of Henry's best hunting and drinking buddies, and Henry made him Archbishop in full expectancy that he would toe the royal line. However, for Henry, it was like booking a holiday in Ibiza with your best mate only to discover that he's become a born-again Christian. The two soon fell out and Beckett spent 5 years in exile before the two patched things up. However, Beckett soon returned to his uncompromising and impractical attitudes. He was one of those insufferable prigs who seem intent on a glorious martyrdom, a fate that 4 over-eager knights provided for him by hacking him to pieces in Canterbury Cathedral.

Like Elvis, death was a good career move for Thomas, as he achieved the sainthood he had so desperately striven for. The chapel where he was murdered became a place of pilgrimage for those who couldn't afford the more expensive trips to Jerusalem or Santiago De Compostella in Spain.

The Royal Arms of Henry II

Henry was born the eldest son of Matilda, the daughter of Henry I, by her second marriage to Geoffrey, Count of Anjou shortly after Matilda had lost out to her cousin Stephen in her struggle to gain the English throne. During the civil war that plunged England into anarchy, she had briefly occupied London, but Matilda had proved so arrogant and obnoxious that the Londoners wisely threw her out.

Henry and Eleanor – together in death, as they had never been in life.

Nonetheless, the family maintained its claim to the English throne andthe young Henry strengthened his position by in 1152, marrying the wealthiest heiress in Europe, Eleanor of Aquitaine.

11 years his senior. Eleanor had only recently been divorced from King Louis VII of France. Finding the pious and religious Louis insufficiently manly, Eleanor had scandalised society by blatantly taking a series of lovers whilst she and Louis were on crusade in the Holy Land. Henry was not particularly regal himself. He was of short, stocky build, with a freckled

the English throne considerably enhanced his attractiveness to the ambitious and canny Eleanor.

In 1153 Henry and a small party of knights landed in England ready to fight for his claim to the throne. The subsequent death in a shipwreck of King Stephen's only son left the king with no stomach for a fight, and he duly granted the succession to Henry. With Stephen's death the following year, Henry was crowned King. His Anjou inheritance, the Aquitaine lands that he accrued through marriage to Eleanor, and now the possession of England, made him the greatest magnate in Europe. However, it would take all of Henry's considerable energy and determination to keep his vast domains under control.

It proved a classic case of overstretch. No sooner had he brought the querulous English magnates to heel than he had to deal with revolts by his French subjects, egged on by his great rival King Louis. Henry spent 20 out of the 34 years of his long reign on the continent, averaging 2,000 miles a year on horseback as he strove to keep his lands intact

In his later years he also had to contend with the intrigues of his own sons, aided by Eleanor, grown vindictive and resentful because of Henry's constant philandering with other women. Following a failed revolt in 1173/4 Henry kept Eleanor under house arrest until his own death released her. When Henry wished to grant Aquitaine to his son John, his eldest son Richard grew resentful and allied with the young French King Phillipe II, whom many believed was Richard's homosexual lover. John's resentment against his father was no doubt exacerbated by Henry's fathering 4 illegitimate children by Richard's fiancée Princess Alice, the French king's sister.

Richard and Louis eventually harried the exhausted and over-worked Henry to his death in 1189, at the age of 66. No better symbol for Henry's reign exists than the mural he had painted in the royal palace at Winchester of an eagle having his eyes pecked out by his own offspring.

The life of Henry II is a classic example of being careful about what you wish for. He married the rich heiress, won the golden crown, and then wore himself out in a vain attempt to keep it all together. In the end it was his wife Eleanor who triumphed. Released from her long captivity, it was she who got to rule the Angevin empire while her son Richard frittered his inheritance away, cutting a dash in the crusades

CAST

WILL

CHRIS PARHAM

Chris is from London and has been in Tokyo since mid 2004. In January he made his Tokyo debut as Trofimov in The Cherry Orchard at the T.A.C. Since then he has operator the lights on numerous productions and during the summer he reprised a version of Howard Barker's Judith at the Etcetera Theatre in London. Chris's next production will be directing Death of a Salesman at Akasaka V Theatre in March

SARAH

NAOKO SHEENA

After a few fringe theatre productions in Tokyo and at the Edinburgh Festival, Naoko Sheena trained at Webber Douglas Academy of Dramatic Arts in London. Her theatre credits in London include Scout in POPCORN, and Arcardina in THE SEAGULL. In Tokyo she has appeared in several TIP shows including Diana in LEND ME A TENOR, Tuptim in THE KING AND I and Sonia in GODSPELL. Her TV credits include the drama series KIMI O MIAGETE and the recently broadcast IKINOKORE (Survive) on NHK 1

KEVIN

MARTIN BURNS

Martin hails from Glasgow in Scotland where he began his acting career at the tender age of 18 and has worked extensively in theatre, radio, TV and Film, throughout the UK and the odd (sometimes VERY odd), tour in Europe for the last 19 years. Since moving to Japan in 2003 he has been trying to get started all over again. His first foray came with Tokyo International Players and their adaptation of Hamlet where he played Polonius. He is very excited to be part of this project!

ERIC

ANTUN PERCEC

Possibly the only British/Croatian/Canadian actor in Japan. Antun was seen on stage in Tokyo in "A Soldier's Tale" where he played "The King" with the company Otono Atorie for the Tokyo 2000 Arts Festival, his professional Shakespeare theatre credits include **Hamlet, A Midsummer Nights Dream, Measure for Measure, "The Merchant of Venice"** and Guildenstern in "**Rosencranz and Guildenstern are Dead**" (Tom Stoppard actually) all in Canada, Neil Simon's **"Plaza Suite"** in Copenhagen Denmark, and Harold Pinter's **"No Man's Land**," he also toured the USA, England, and Ireland with the Renaissance Theatre Company "**Poculi Ludeque Societas,"** Film and TV credits include "**Nobody Makes me Cry**," Friday's Curse," and "**Krieghof.**" Also TV commercials in Canada, Denmark and Japan.

BOB

PATRICK SMITH

Patrick was born and raised in London until the age of 8 when his family moved to Australia. Patrick has already had a long career in the creative arts. He plays guitar, bass, drums, piano, violin, sings and has performed on stage and television in Australia

Patrick has lived in Tokyo for two years and is the head of International Capital Markets at a leading international law firm where he advises the world's largest investment banks. In addition to being a lawyer, Patrick is also a qualified psychologist.

SAM

CHRISTINE BISHARD

Christine Bishard has worked with some of the worlds largest international corporations, training management in presentations, rhetoric and verbal skills. A native Californian, Christine travelled extensively and worked in every aspect of training before eventually settling in Japan, the home of her maternal grandmother.

This is Christine's first play.

TIM

LAZ BREZER

Laz Brezer (Canada) has performed as a professional musician and actor, and as a dancer, in both his own solo productions and in works of prominent choreographers for the past 35 years. Laz moved to Japan in 1991, where he has a holistic healing practice based in Cranio-sacral Therapy, Feldenkrais Method, and Compassionate Cognitive Counselling.

Teddy

REBECCA ROMANS

Rebecca Romans has worked on stage or behind the scenes in many theatricalTeddy productions. In 2005 she was Roxy in Tokyo Theatre for Children's Production of Sleeping Beauty. She currently tours Japan in a Children's Magic Show for World Family Club. " Its very exciting to work in theatre as a production evolves or as Will says: " Becoming the Words." "

Nathan

MICHAEL MITCHELL

Despite the early disappointment of not being adopted by Madonna, Michael's Anglo-Malawian lineage led him from Canada to Canterbury, Bombay to Brasilia and, following an undergraduate stint at the LSE, which netted him a law degree, he moved to Japan. Michael debuted on stage at age eleven, as Willy Wonka in the school play. His literary repertoire includes playing Oberon, Teen Angel, Orsino, and the Genie, but still firmly believes that Seyton is a character in Dante's Inferno.

Lovitz

BOB WERLEY

Bob was born and raised in the U.S. but has called Tokyo home for the past 5 years. A dedicated theatre man he has acted in over 30 plays in 3 countries. Some of his favourite moments came from being the Gorilla in Cabaret to being typecast as Slender in The Merry Wives of Windsor. In Tokyo he played Miles in The Drawer Boy with the Sometimes Y Theatre. He has also been involved in numerous productions with TIP, including playing William Blore in *And Then There Were None* this October at the Tokyo American Club. Also, keep an eye out for him with the Tokyo Comedy Store at the Crocodile in Shibuya and in Christmas' *Moon Over Buffalo.*

Shakespeare

The Droeshout portrait from the first folio

We actually know very little about Shakespeare's life for certain, but what we do know has been gathered by scholars and academics from court and other clerical records. The first 20 years of his life is very scant in detail but we do know he was born in 1564, probably on April 23, though no birth register exists but we do have a record of his baptism on April 26, 1564. The fact that Shakespeare died on April 23, 52 years later, has led many to believe his birth and death both occurred on that same date. At age 18 (1582), William married Anne Hathaway, a local farmer's daughter eight years his senior. Their first daughter (Susanna) was born six months later (1583), and twins Judith and Hamnet were born in 1585.

It is estimated that Shakespeare arrived in London around 1588 and began to establish himself as an actor and playwright. Evidently, Shakespeare garnered envy early on for his talent, as related by the critical attack of Robert Greene, a London playwright, in 1592: "...an upstart crow, beautified with our feathers, that with his Tiger's heart wrapped in a player's hide, supposes he is as well able to bombast out a blank verse as the best of you: and being an absolute Johannes factotum, is in his own conceit the only Shake-scene in a country."

The Chandos portrait
Attributed to Joseph Taylor circa 1630

When, in 1592, the Plague closed the theatres for about two years, Shakespeare turned to writing book-length narrative poetry. Most notable were "Venus and Adonis" and "The Rape of Lucrece," both of which were dedicated to the Earl of Southampton, whom scholars accept as Shakespeare's friend and benefactor despite a lack of documentation. During this same period, Shakespeare was writing his sonnets, which are more likely signs of the time's fashion rather than actual love poems detailing any particular relationship. He returned to play writing when theatres reopened in 1594, and published no more poetry. His sonnets were published without his consent in 1609, shortly before his retirement.

The Globe Theatre London

Amid all of his success, Shakespeare suffered the loss of his only son, Hamnet, who died in 1596 at the age of 11. But Shakespeare's career continued unabated and in London in 1599, he became one of the partners in the new Globe Theatre built by the Chamberlain's Men.

When Queen Elizabeth died in 1603 and was succeeded by her cousin King James of Scotland, the Chamberlain's Men was renamed the King's Men, and Shakespeare's productivity and popularity continued uninterrupted. He invested in London real estate and, one year away from retirement, purchased a second theatre, the Blackfriars Gatehouse, in partnership with his fellow actors, included among whom was Richard Burbage. His final play was

Henry VIII, two years before his death in 1616. Incredibly, most of Shakespeare's plays had never been published in anything except pamphlet form, and were simply extant as acting scripts stored at the Globe. Only the efforts of two of Shakespeare's company, John Heminges and Henry Condell, preserved his 36 plays (minus Pericles, the thirty-seventh) in the First Folio. Heminges and Condell published the plays, they said, "only to keep the memory of so worthy a friend and fellow alive as was our Shakespeare". Theatre scripts were not regarded as literary works of art, but only the basis for the performance. Plays were a popular form of entertainment for all layers of society in Shakespeare's time, which perhaps explains why Hamlet feels compelled to instruct the travelling Players on the fine points of acting, urging them not *"to split the ears of the groundlings,"* nor *"speak no more than is set down for them."* Hamlet Act 3 Scene 2

Holy Trinity Church
Stratford Upon Avon

Present copies of Shakespeare's plays have, in some cases, been reconstructed in part from scripts written down by various members of an acting company who performed particular roles. Shakespeare's plays, like those of many of the actors who also were playwrights, belonged to the acting company. The performance, rather than the script, was what concerned the author, for that was how his play would become popular—and how the company, in which many actors were shareholders, would make money.

William Shakespeare died on April 23, 1616, and was buried two days later in the chancel of Holy Trinity Church where he had been baptized exactly 52 years earlier.

William Shakespeare's legacy is a body of work that will never again be equalled in Western civilization. His words have endured for 400 years, and still reach across the centuries as powerfully as ever. Even in death, he leaves a final piece of verse as his epitaph:

Good friend, for Jesus' sake forbeare
To dig the dust enclosed here.
Blessed be the man that spares these stones,
And cursed be he that moves my bones.

By Matrin Burns

CUT SCENES

Performed in Tokyo in 2006, the original production of the play contained an extra act, providing motivation for Bob's inclusion in the deception.

Although enjoyable, it was regarded superfluous to the overall structure of the play and was cut from subsequent performances in an effort to curtail the two hour thirty minute run time.

It is presented here for the first time outside the Tokyo performance.

ACT 3

CURTAIN UP.

THE CURTAIN RISES ON A CONSERVATIVE GEN-TLEMEN'S CLUB DEEP IN THE HEART OF NEW YORK. THE DECOR IS OLD ENGLISH STYLE: WING-BACKED LEATHER ARMCHAIRS AROUND OPEN FIREPLACES AND BOOKCASES.

TWO CHARACTERS, TEDDY AND NATHAN, SIT CENTRE ROOM SPEAKING SILENTLY TO EACH OTHER. A BUNNY GIRL DRESSED IN SEXY LINGE-RIE STYLE ATTIRE SERVES THEM BRANDY AND CIGARS.

ENTER FOOL STAGE LEFT.

FOOL (SINGING)   If I were a rich man, biddy biddy biddy, biddy biddy biddy, biddy biddy bum, I guess I join a club like this one, if I were a wealthy man. Ha!

SEEING THE AUDIENCE HE STOPS.

You came back! We did not think you would.

The acts were long, and not so good.

But this! Ah, this I'd make my home

For here the rich men build their Rome.

HE LOOKS AROUND.

Such opulence, such wine, cigars,

You would not find in English Bars!

No one can join, you must be asked,

A secret handshake gets you past

To a room where rich men choose your fate

At five percent the interest rate.

They sit, discuss the Dow, the yen

Not only gods play chess with men.

TEDDY   (UPON RECEIVING A LIGHT FOR HIS CIGAR FROM THE FOOL.) Thank you, honey. (TO

THE OTHER MAN) No, simply all I said to him was, Greenspan! Six months later he was out on his ear.

NATHAN   Then it's not true.

TEDDY   Oh, it's true, of course it's true. Every damn word of it is true. That's the point of the whole thing. I just didn't say it in words, that's all.

NATHAN   Ah.

TEDDY   Market forces. And we're the ones pushing it.

NATHAN   (LAUGHING AT THE BON MOT) Say it with shares, I always say.

TEDDY   Exactly. I tell you, words are yesterday's thing. Hell, they were my grandmother's thing. Anyone can do words. They're dead, I tell you. It's money that talks and the market's the mouthpiece.

NATHAN   I couldn't agree with you more.

TEDDY   I foresee a time, in our lifetime if we've got anything to say about it, (NATHAN LAUGHS) when we'll have forgotten how to say anything at all. Words will be as dead to us as…

NATHAN   Greenspan?

TEDDY   Exactly so. Everything will be numbers. Displeasure, rhetoric and a good fuck will all be displayed by the movement of money. Numbers, sliding silently to display, well, us, I suppose.

NATHAN   Sounds perfection.

TEDDY   We'll all be IPO's by then, of course. Each person limited on the Dow. You're angry with someone, you ditch their stock. Like them, you'll buy it. Catch my drift?

NATHAN   Exactly.

TEDDY   Won't even need to order. You'll just give the waiter money and he'll return with whatever it covers.

NATHAN   Imagine. Coleridge as a series of ones and zeros.

TEDDY   Nathan, Nathan. Nate. Not binary. Monetary! Coleridge would be pounds. Heavy and overbearing. Whitman's dollars. Shakespeare, yen.

NATHAN   Hmm?

TEDDY   Overvalued. A run on the baht and we could do away with Jane Austen once and for all.

NATHAN   And wouldn't that be a fine thing?

TEDDY   Bloody BBC.

THE SIDE DOOR OPENS AND BOB WALKS IN STAGE LEFT, A MANUSCRIPT UNDER HIS ARM, THROWING HIS COAT AT THE BUNNY GIRL AS HE MAKES HIS WAY OVER.

TEDDY SEES HIM.

TEDDY   (SOTTO) What is he wearing?

NATHAN   (TURNING) Hmm?

BOB   Gentlemen! (HE WAVES THE MANUSCRIPT) I have it! (TO BUNNY) Scotch, please.

SHE TURNS TO GO, AND UNBIDDEN AND UNWANTED HE PULLS UP A CHAIR AND SITS NEXT TO THEM.

EXIT BUNNY.

NATHAN   You seem excited, Robert. Got yourself another wife, have you?

HE LAUGHS AT HIS OWN JOKE, NOBODY JOINING HIM.

BOB   Better. (TO TEDDY) Tell me Teddy. You run, what, most of the press on the eastside. One of them must have come up with this sometime. What's a man – a person – want out of life?

TEDDY   Whatever I've got, I suppose.

BOB   (IMPRESSED AT THE ANSWER) Ah, see, there's that education. That's where it comes in handy!

The comeback. I missed that, see. Left school when I was fifteen. Feel I should have stayed on, you know? Couple more years and I'd be able to have a comeback like that. What do you think?

NATHAN   Perhaps it's in the blood.

BOB   Nah, I get mine tested. (TO TEDDY) Tell me. You get tickets for that Lyceum thing last week?

NATHAN   M.N.D.?

BOB   What? No. One before that.

TEDDY   The Last Promiscuity? No. I read a review about it in one of my papers though. Didn't miss a thing. Why? You thinking of going into vaudeville?

BOB   Something like that.

ENTER BUNNY

BUNNY RE-ENTERS CARRYING A TRAY WITH A SCOTCH AND CIGAR FOR BOB. INSTEAD OF HEADING OVER TO THEM THOUGH, SHE TAKES CENTRE STAGE AND ADDRESSES THE AUDIENCE. THE OTHER CHARACTERS TURN TO WATCH HER, AS THOUGH IT'S NOT PART OF THE PLAY. AMAZED SHE'S DOING IT.

BUNNY   You'd think, dressed like this, that I wouldn't have an opinion on propriety, but I do. See, this may look ridiculous on me and it's hardly the most comfortable thing you can wear. But the tips! Ah, the tips you get for it are fantastic. And, I'm not talking tens and twenties here. Hundreds. Thousands!

I used to model, and let me tell you, that was far more degrading. Far more. Half the time your tits are out. Half the time you're frozen somewhere on a beach. Least they keep the heat on in here.

I don't strip. I don't dance. I bring drinks, I smile politely and light their cigars. All there is to it really. So they pat me on the hiney now and again. They stare at my boobs. So what? People been doing that to me since I was fifteen!

(SHE MOTIONS TO BOB) See that guy over there. One of the girls married him! Seriously! I mean, I know we're not supposed to think like that and all, but, seriously!

And what is it? Showmanship! Nothing more. So I'm dressed as a rabbit! So what? It's all a little fantasy. All a little titillation for the old folk. All it is. Mostly they're good. There's strict rules about sex and that, so none of them do anything. They just want, what? To role-play! It's like Disney. You get dressed up as Winnie the Pooh, you get dressed up as rabbit. Really! It's just a character. Same as any other! And the one thing I've learnt in my time is that we're all just characters. All of us! You included. We're just one person sitting in a theatre watching everyone else up here on the stage. Right now you're characters in the life of the person sitting next to you. You're characters in mine! We all want.. hell, we try to make people the characters we want. Make them act like we want, make them do what we want. We're all trying to make ourselves a happy ending. What's wrong with that? So don't judge me. I'm just serving drinks.

SHE MOVES OFF, SLOWLY CIRCLING THE CHARACTERS AND UNEASILY, THE THREE CONTINUE WITH THEIR CONVERSATIONS.

TEDDY   I almost hesitate to ask, Robert, but what is it you have there?

BOB   (HE THROWS THE MANUSCRIPT DOWN ONTO THE TABLE IN FRONT OF THEM) This!

TEDDY   (WITHOUT LOOKING AT IT) A screenplay? Really.

BOB   A brand new play by William Shakespeare!

NATHAN LEANS FORWARD AND PICKS IT UP, IN-
TERESTED.

NATHAN   Oh, I read him at L.S.E.

TEDDY   Robert, Shakespeare's been dead for about
five hundred years. Whatever you've got there is hardly
likely to be a new play.

NATHAN   (READING) Henry the Second. Not sure
I read this one.

BOB   You haven't. Like I told you. It's new.

NATHAN   Wasn't he the one with the limp?

TEDDY   (EXASPERATED AND TIRED OF THE
CONVERSATION) Robert, I'm sure that whatever you
have here is riveting but Nathan and I were in the middle
of discussing a rather important political problem so…

BUNNY DELIVERS BOB'S DRINK.

BOB   Thank you, honey. (TO TEDDY) Screw politics.
Screw politics Teddy, and screw your if-you-don't-mind
while you're at it.

TEDDY   Really, Robert! Must you bring the street
in with you?

BOB   You know there's not a political rung on the ladder I didn't grease for you. I make more money in a week
than you in a month, and I've been to the White House
five times this year to your three.

TEDDY   Yes, but I declined the last four. Really,
Robert, if we're going to compare manhoods then I insist
on your doctor being present. I'm really not sure your
heart can stand it. (HE LOOKS LASCIVIOUSLY AT
BUNNY) What with that little wife of your's.

NATHAN   You know, this is actually pretty good.
Very on and off, of course. Obviously one of his earlier
works.

BOB   Somewhere around Wednesday, I think.

NATHAN   More Cressida than Macbeth and he drivels on somewhat, but that's Shakespeare for you.

TEDDY   Nathan. Whatever you're talking about, stop it. That's not Shakespeare.

NATHAN   It's not? Really? Could never keep up with the Kings.

BOB   How long have we known each other, Teddy? You and me?

TEDDY   You're boring me Robert. And I earn too much to be bored.

BOB   I'd like to make you a bet.

TEDDY   I don't bet. Except on chess. You play chess Robert? No. Craps isn't it?

BOB   You'll make this one.

TEDDY   I doubt it.

NATHAN   I can see it now. The metre's all wrong. No iambic pentameter. I mean it's there, then it isn't, if you catch my meaning.

BOB   Who was it founded this club, Teddy? Your great-grandfather wasn't it? Endless glass ceilings for you to smash through.

TEDDY   Am I to be lectured?

BOB   You got it all sewn up, don't you? And I don't blame you for it. You're an elitist bitch …

TEDDY   (LAUGHING) Really!

BOB   …who… No, really. No money like old money, right? And you can't stand it, can you? That they let me in here? I got no schooling. I got no class. Just a goddamned checkbook and you hate me for it.

TEDDY   Robert. Robert! I invited you to join. Remember?

BOB   And made me pay through the nose for it.

NATHAN   (TAKING UMBRAGE) What's going on here, Robert? Teddy and I were having a quiet little chat. What is this thing?

BOB   Nathan, I'll tell you. What you have in your hands is a one hundred percent new – not forged, not rewritten – new play by William Shakespeare. And I'm putting it on at the Lyceum next month.

NATHAN   And why on earth would you do that?

BOB   Why? To see if anyone notices, of course!

NATHAN   I'm not with you.

TEDDY   Nathan, Robert thinks he's got himself a coup de théâtre. Isn't that right, Robert? A little surprise something with which to win our awe and respect. Playing on the naïveté of the general… produce, thus showing himself to be a true bel-esprit of our age. Is that it, Robert?

NATHAN   Well, I wouldn't have thought he'd have much trouble in that!

BOB   Not the, how did you say, produce? Not them. You, Teddy. I want to put one over on you.

TEDDY   Really, old boy? Well, you shouldn't have tipped the wink, so to speak. Cat's out of the bag and all that.

BOB   You're right. I know. I thought to myself. If Teddy can't tell this is a genuine Shakespeare, who could? And if Teddy was left with egg on his face… Man, what a sight.

TEDDY   Et tu.

BOB   But then I thought. That's not how to beat Teddy. And I'm opening up here! That's what I want to do. I want to beat you! So I thought to myself. What does Teddy love more than his prize-winning intellect, hmm? Money. Money! And more to the point, winning money from me! So, I'll make you a bet. I will bet you, here and now, that not one – I repeat, not one - journalist, not one socialite, not one man in the print, public or porno-fucking-graphic media – that you largely own – can tell the goddamned difference between this (HE HOLDS UP

THE MANUSCRIPT) and the real thing. There it is. On the table. A bet.

TEDDY   Not interested.

BOB   No? Let's make it interesting then.

TEDDY   What have you possibly got that I can't have.

BOB   Two things. First there's my wife.

TEDDY   What makes you think I want your wife?

BOB   Nathan wants her, don't you Nathan?

TEDDY   Robert, your wife may well be a glorious creature but (HE GESTURES AT BUNNY) glorious creatures are a dime a dozen. Why would I want your... pablum.

BOB   Because I love her.

TEDDY   And she you?

BOB   Does it matter?

TEDDY   I see. And the second thing?

BOB   (REACHING INTO HIS POCKET AND PULL-ING OUT A SHEET OF PAPER) This.

TEDDY LOOKS AT THE PAPER BUT DOESN'T MOVE TO PICK IT UP.

TEDDY   Which is?

BOB   My ten percent stake in your company.

TEDDY   Nonsense. Only Gray has that large a holding.

BOB   You should pay more attention. I've been buying for months now. A name here, a corporation there. Completely illegal of course, but proving it could bankrupt you. Gray offered me two for the whole lot this morning. Of course, he'd have a controlling stake if he got another ten, and two is about a third of the money I paid to get them. But you know, I'm tempted. Tempted.

TEDDY   (SERIOUS NOW) And if you win?

NATHAN   Hang on Teddy, you're not seriously considering…

TEDDY   Quiet, Nathan. What happens if you win?

BOB   (SMILING) The chair comes up in the fall, doesn't it? I mean. You're a lock, of course. Been your's for, what? Fifty years?

TEDDY   I see.

BOB   Thirty, then. But with your backing, you know what, I think I could do well in it. My very own club! Well, chair anyway. Think what I could do. Think of the contacts! Or I could open the doors. Hell, let anyone with a billion in. Gates still looking to get membership, isn't he? Think of what I could do with the place.

TEDDY   Alright. Sell them to me now and I'll back you for the chair in the fall.

NATHAN   Hang on, Teddy!

TEDDY   Stay out of this, Nathan. This is for the big boys now.

BOB   No.

TEDDY   Cost price and the club. A hell of a deal.

BOB   I want to beat you Teddy.

TEDDY   You may lose. Not everyone is as stupid as we think they are.

BOB   (MOTIONING TO NATHAN) He believed it.

TEDDY   (SMILING) Well…

BOB   I want to beat you, Teddy. But more importantly, (HE TAPS THE MANUSCRIPT) I want him to beat you.

TEDDY   And he is?

BOB   Nobody. A man in a shit marriage with a shit wife, living in a one room apartment probably, worrying about how he's going to pay the goddamned electricity bill. He's nothing. Not to me, not to you. Doubt he's published a goddamned thing in his goddamned life, and I want him to beat you. Him! And not in the market. Not with money, Teddy. I don't want to beat you with money.

Words! I want him to beat you with words. Just scribblings on paper. Hey, like the ones you own! Go figure.

TEDDY   This is about Viacom, isn't it?

BOB   This is about fun, Teddy. Fun.

TEDDY   (CONSIDERING) I see. And how do you know I won't cheat. Just drop a hint here or there. It's easy enough. Nathan might. Chat to my editor.

BOB   Nah. I'd know. Then I'd just give them to Gray. Anyway. You wouldn't do that.

TEDDY   Wouldn't I?

BOB   No. We're too much alike, you and me, Teddy.

TEDDY   We're absolutely nothing alike, (WITH DISDAIN) Bob.

BOB   Oh, we are. We both know life, you and me. We both know how to play it. We're not above cheating. Hell, how'd you think I got these stocks in the first place? But when it's personal – and this is personal – Teddy, when it's personal we both know that cheating kind of takes the life out of it. Doesn't it? I beat you. You beat me. Ten years down the line the other one will be back. That's what living's for. Course, that's if either of us have got ten years left in us.

TEDDY   We are monoliths, Bob. We'll live forever! Well, one of us will. Just so we're clear. If this… thing… goes on…

BOB   It'll go on. I'll make sure of it.

TEDDY   I take it you're billing it as a reworking?

BOB   Naturally.

TEDDY   And if no one in the media notices…

BOB   Which they won't.

TEDDY   Including my lot…

BOB   Especially you Teddy. Especially your lot.

TEDDY   Then I give you the chair. But! And we're clear on this.

BOB   Like raindrops.

TEDDY   If there's so much as one article in any paper, mine or otherwise, stipulating that the whole thing is a hoax.

BOB   Go on.

TEDDY   You return my shares and your wife goes back to serving me drinks.

BOB   (CAUTIOUS) That wasn't the deal.

TEDDY   I changed it. Let's just say it's how I choose to have her, shall we. She remains your wife, of course, but she brings me drinks, lights my cigars, and Nathan touches her up now and again. When the mood's right.

BOB   Then I take it we have a deal.

TEDDY   We have a deal.

THE TWO SHAKE HANDS.

TEDDY (CONT.)   What makes you so sure you're going to win?

BOB   People believe what I want them to believe. Always have done.

TEDDY   All of the people, all of the time?

BOB   Just the ones I'm talking to.

HE GETS UP AND HANDS HIS DRINK TO BUNNY, WHO HANDS HIM HIS COAT AS THOUGH SHE'S BEEN EXPECTING HIM TO LEAVE.

NATHAN   When is it, anyway?

BOB   A month from now. Want me to save you some tickets?

NATHAN   If you wouldn't mind. Always been rather partial to Shakespeare.

BOB   Well you'll have to buy them online like everyone else. Teddy'll help you.

NATHAN   Goodbye Robert. A fool and his women are soon parted.

BOB   Must be why you're not married then. (LAUGH-

ING SLIGHTLY) Whatdayaknow! Must have learnt some education, after all. (HE GOES TO LEAVE) Teddy.

NATHAN   Robert.

EXIT BOB STAGE LEFT.

NATHAN (CONT. TO TEDDY) Did I tell you I did Macbeth at the Fringe?

TEDDY   Really Nathan? I didn't think anyone did much of anything useful in the UK anymore.

END OF ACT 3.

The character of TEDDY returns during the final act revealing the deception to Sarah.

Fitting roughly into Page 67 of this book, the scene originally unfolded as follows.

THERE'S A KNOCK AT THE DOOR. EVERYONE LOOKS UP AT IT. IT REPEATS, HARDER.

ERIC   That'll be Scene-Cutter. Better let him in.

HE LOOKS AT BOB WHO NODS BEFORE GOING OVER TO THE DOOR AND OPENING IT.

ENTER TEDDY UPSTAGE.

EFFORTLESSLY TEDDY ENTERS, ERIC STEPPING ASIDE, EASILY INTIMIDATED BY THE MAN'S PRESENCE.

TEDDY STOPS AND LOOKS AROUND.

TEDDY   Well, this takes me back.

BOB   Teddy! Schlepping?

TEDDY   Robert. Well, I just had to come and see for myself. A troubadour's cave. Most fitting!

WILL   (STEPPING FORWARD, CONFUSED) Mr Williams? It's a pleasure.

TEDDY   (TAKING THE PROFFERED HAND AND SHAKING) You know me?

WILL   Certainly.

TEDDY   Well, you must be the young bard. I have to say, I was amused by the whole thing. Very amused.
(WILL LOOKS AT BOB AND BOB NODS ASSENT)
WILL   Thank you. (CONFUSED) I think.
TEDDY   You should. I was… Hmm… I don't know what I was expecting. Some Bible references or something, but there were whole scenes in there, no? Did I perhaps catch a whiff of Pericles?
WILL   You know your Shakespeare.
TEDDY   New York, it seems, does not. Hmm? Still, very amusing (HE TURNS TO BOB) Robert. Panegyric offerings. I underestimated you.
SAM STEPS UP AND PUTS AN ARM AROUND BOB PROTECTIVELY.
BOB   I believe you've met Samantha. My wife.
TEDDY   (TAKING HER HAND) My dear, you were simply glorious. What can one say? Glorious. My losses tonight are indeed great.
SAM   Thanks.
TEDDY   Ah.
BOB PULLS AN ENVELOPE FROM HIS POCKET AND HANDS IT TO TEDDY.
TEDDY   What's this?
 BOB   A contract.
TEDDY   May I ask?
BOB   Shares in CNB. Market price. I don't want Chris to get them anymore than you do.
TEDDY   (TAKEN ABACK BUT PUTTING THE ENVELOPE INTO HIS POCKET NONETHELESS) I should not have been so gracious.
BOB   Yeah.
TEDDY   Well. (LOOKING AROUND) It seems there is quite a merry band here. (ADDRESSING AT LARGE) Congratulations to you all. Quite a perfor-

mance. I will have to fire my editors at once. (THERE'S A LAUGH) Hmm. Yes. At any rate. My hat is off to you. You have proved once more that the average and above average alike are no more well-read than an Iranian Prince. I insist on buying you all drinks!

KEVIN STEPS FORWARD.

KEVIN   May I say…

ENTER SARAH UPSTAGE THROUGH THE NOW UNLOCKED DOOR AND WALKS ACROSS THE ROOM UNNOTICED.

TEDDY   I'm sure you may. But get me a drink first. Whisky, if you have it.

SARAH TAPS WILL ON THE SHOULDER AND WHEN HE TURNS TO SEE HER SHE KISSES HIM PASSIONATELY, HER PREVIOUS ANIMOSITY LOST. WILL PULLS AWAY.

WILL   Mmmm. Hey. I thought you were up-stairs.

SARAH   I wanted to be with you.

WILL   I was just…

SARAH   They love it! Even Daddy thinks it's good. I'm proud of you. (WILL LOOKS AWKWARD) What?

WILL   You're proud of me?

SARAH   Of course! It's a success.

WILL   And that's the measure of it, is it?

SARAH   What do you mean.

TEDDY COMES ACROSS.

TEDDY   This must be your good wife?

WILL   Mr. Williams, may I introduce Sarah.

SARAH   (SHAKING A PROFFERED HAND) Ted Williams? CNB Ted Williams?

TEDDY   Teddy, please.

WILL   Mr. Williams was in the audience tonight.

He asked to join us for…

SARAH   It's an honour.

TEDDY   Quite. Your husband has outdone himself, Mrs. Burrows.

SARAH   It's… Thank you.

TEDDY   I've never been a writer but, I know a couple and there's one thing that marks a good writer from a bad one. A complete lack of perspective.

SARAH   You've… I'm sorry, you've read Will's work?

WILL   Ah.

TEDDY   Read? No. But I saw it tonight. Heard it, rather.

SARAH   Mr. Williams. I'm sorry. Will didn't wri… You mean the edit?

TEDDY   Oh, dear. (TO WILL) She doesn't know?

WILL   No.

SARAH   Know?

TEDDY   (IGNORING HER) Who does, per se?

WILL   Everyone here.

TEDDY   No one else?

WILL   Just us.

SARAH   Know what?

TEDDY   Well, well. I must say. That is something.

SARAH   I'm sorry. I don't understand.

TEDDY   My dear lady. Your husband is the perpetrator of the biggest hoax on the New York public since Livedoor went public.

SARAH   I'm… What?

TEDDY   Mrs. Burrows. Your husband wrote this play.

SARAH   He wrote it?

WILL   Sarah…

TEDDY   Every word of it. Well, not every word. He

stole some lines from Shakespeare himself, but…

WILL   Sarah.

SARAH   Mr Williams. I'm afraid you don't seem to understand. Are you saying that… (TURNING TO WILL) Will, what is he saying?

TEDDY   Your husband wrote the play.

SARAH   Shakespeare!

TEDDY   No.

SARAH   But I read it in school.

TEDDY   Hmm. Perhaps this is something the pair of you need to discuss privately.

WILL   Sarah…

SARAH   Mr. Williams. I'm sorry. I mean, don't get me wrong here, Will directed this. But it's a Shakespeare play.

BOB GOES OVER TO LOVITZ AS HE ENTERS UP-STAGE, BLOCKING HIS WAY.

WILL   I wrote it.

BOB   Private party.

LOVITZ PULLS OUT A CARD AND HANDS IT TO BOB.

SARAH   On a level, sure…

TEDDY EXCUSES HIMSELF.

WILL   On paper.

BOB   Really? (LOVITZ NODS AND BOB WAVES HIM IN)

SARAH   It's a Shakespeare play!

WILL   (SOTTO) It's not. Really. I wrote it.

SARAH   I read it in school! I did a paper on it!

Continued on Page 73.

Also by

THOMAS ALEXANDER

THOMAS ALEXANDER

THE VISITOR

THE VISITOR

BY

THOMAS ALEXANDER

WHEN THE LOVER OF A FAMOUS
WRITER GOES MISSING IN A WAR
RAVAGED COUNTRY, HE BRIBES HIS
WAY INTO A JAIL TO QUESTION HER
HUSBAND, A MISSIONARY, WHO
IS BEING TORTURED AS A TRAIN-
ING EXERCISE BY HIS CAPTORS.

ALONE IN THE CELL, THE TWO
START A DIALOGUE ABOUT THE
NATURE OF BELIEF.

BELIEF IN GOD, LOVE AND POLITICS.

MURDER ME GENTLY

By

THOMAS ALEXANDER

"ONE MAN... ONE WOMAN... AND THE QUEST FOR JUSTICE IN AN UNJUST WORLD"

MODERN DAY RUSSIA THROUGH THE MEDIUM OF FILM NOIR

BLENDING REAL LIFE EVENTS WITH COMEDY AND INTRIGUE, *MURDER ME GENTLY*'S UNIQUE PERSPECTIVE ON THE WORLD OF RUSSIAN POLITICS AS SEEN THROUGH THE LENS OF FLIM NOIR, SPANS THE ASSASINATION OF INTERNATIONALLY RENOWNED JOURNALISTS, PUTIN'S REACH FOR THE RETURN OF SOVIET SATELITE STATES, AND THE INFLITRATION OF GOVERNMENT BY OLIGARCHS AND CRIMINALS.

PROVIDING A DAMMING INDICTMENT OF THE WEST'S INABILITY TO HALT MOSCOW'S POLICY OF EXPANSIONISM *MURDER ME GENTLY* LENDS A THEATRICAL EXPOSE TO THE VERY REAL WORLD OF CORRUPTION AND GREED IN INTERNATIONAL POLITICS TODAY.

A CONMAN, A DISGRACED INTERPOL AGENT, A MAFIA BOSS, A CIA SPOOK, AND THE SECRET TO THE FUTURE ALL UNITE IN AN UNLIKELY ALLIANCE IN A LOVE AFFAIR THAT WILL DEFINE THE FATE OF THE WORLD IN THOMAS ALEXANDER'S

... MURDER ME ... GENTLY!

GRE⋀T

GREAT

BY

THOMAS ALEXANDER

A REMOTE ROOM IN THE THROWS OF WINTER.

THE ONCE GREAT MAN LIVES ALONE NOW WITH HIS SON,

AN OLD FRIEND HAS COME TO VISIT. HE HAS CLIMBED UP FROM THE VILLAGE IN ORDER TO OFFER THE OLD MAN ONE LAST CHANCE TO ESCAPE THE ENCROACHING WINTER THAT IS ABOUT TO TAKE HIM, STIRRING UP MEMORIES OF BETTER TIMES AND THE WARMTH OF SUMMER.

BEGAT

BY

THOMAS ALEXANDER

IN A COUNTRY, AFTER THE WAR, A JUDGE THROWS A DINNER PARTY, SEEKING SUPPORT AGAINST A POWERFUL MINISTER WHO HAS RAPED AND KILLED A SERVANT GIRL.

BUT THE JUDGE HIMSELF IS THE TARGET TONIGHT, AND THE SHADOW OF THE WAR HE SO DESPERATELY WANTS TO LEAVE BEHIND THREATENS TO ENGULF HIS FAMILY AS A YOUNG WOMAN SEEKS REVENGE FOR THE SINS OF HIS PAST.

HAPPINESS

BY

THOMAS ALEXANDER

ON A REMOTE HEADLAND IN NORTH WALES A MAN AND HIS PARAPLEGIC SON DREAM OF LIFE BEYOND THE CONFINES OF THEIR FOUR WALLS.

BUT WHEN A WOMAN OFFERS THEM THE ESCAPE THEY SO CRAVE THEY FIND THEY ARE BOUND BY MORE THEN THEIR DREAMS.

THE JEALOUSY OF A BORED POLICE-MAN AND THE KINDNESS OF A MAIL ORDER BRIDE SET THEM ON A PATH OF HOPE AND DESTRUCTION.

THE LAST CHRISTMAS

IT'S NEWS!

THE LAST CHRISTMAS

BY

THOMAS ALEXANDER

WHEN AN EMBATTLED NEWSROOM RECEIVES A POTENTIALLY EARTH SHATTERING STORY MINUTES BEFORE AIR ON CHRISTMAS DAY THE CAREFUL EQUILIBRIUM OF THE TEAM IS SHATTERED AND OLD DIVIDING LINES COME TO THE FORE, TURNING CO-WORKER AGAINST CO-WORKER.

SET IN REAL TIME AND INCORPORATING ACTUAL AND INTERCHANGEABLE NEWS EVENTS THE LAST CHRISTMAS PITS SOCIAL POLITICS AGAINST JOURNALISTIC INTEGRITY IN A BATTLE OF THE ETHICS.

GOD

BY

THOMAS ALEXANDER

WHEN THE NAMED PARTNER OF A SMALL LAW FIRM DIES, LEAVING LARGE DEBT, THE REMAINING MISFITS OF THE FIRM ARE FORCED TO TAKE ON JUST ABOUT ANY CLIENT AVAILABLE, INCLUDING A LITIGIOUS SOCCER-MUM WHO WOULD LIKE TO SUE GOD FOR THE DEATH OF HER HUSBAND – HIT BY A LIGHTNING BOLT ON THE 15TH HOLE OF A MUNICIPAL GOLF COURSE.

THE TRIAL BECOMES COMPLICATED HOWEVER, WHEN AN INDIGENT WITH NO BACKGROUND AND A CANNY KNACK OF KNOWING EVERYONE'S BACKGROUND ENTERS THE COURTROOM CLAIMING TO BE 'GOD'.

BATTING BACK AND FORE BETWEEN THE COURTROOM AND THE PERSONAL LIVES OF THE LAWYERS, 'GOD' IS A FAST PACED COURTROOM DRAMA/COMEDY THAT USES ORIGINAL STAGING AND NON-LINEAR STORYTELLING TO PROVIDE A LIGHTHEARTED, BUT COMPLEX SOCIAL DRAMA.

THE FAMILY

BY

THOMAS ALEXANDER

TODAY, FOR THE FIRST TIME IN LONGER THAN ANYONE CAN REMEMBER, THE FAMILY ARE GATHERING. THEY ARE GATHERING TO CELEBRATE THE ENGAGEMENT OF THE MATRIARCHAL NIECE, THEY ARE GATHERING TO CELEBRATE THE LAST BIRTHDAY OF THE PATRIARCH, THEY ARE GATHERING TO WELCOME HOME THE PRODIGAL SON AND HIS BEAUTIFUL GIRLFRIEND AND THEY ARE GOING TO CELEBRATE ALL THIS WITH A SLIDE-SHOW.

CANDID PHOTOGRAPHS. PHOTOGRAPHS OF THINGS NO ONE THOUGHT ANYONE ELSE KNEW ABOUT. PHOTOGRAPH TAKEN WHEN NO ONE ELSE WAS THERE.

IT'S ALL COMING OUT TODAY. IN BLACK AND WHITE FOR EVERYONE TO SEE. THE REMNANTS OF CHILD ABUSE, INFIDELITY, LOSS, DESTRUCTION AND MISSED BIRTHDAY PARTIES. IT'S ALL COMING OUT. IT'S GOING TO BE A LONG NIGHT. POSSIBLY FOREVER.

THE RECRUITMENT OFFICER

BY

THOMAS ALEXANDER

TOM, A CHARMING YANKEE RECRUITER, COMES TO AN UNSPECIFIED ENGLISH TOWN AND FALLS IN LOVE WITH THE CONFERENCE CENTRE MANAGER, JULIA.

BUT WHAT EXACTLY IS HE RECRUITING FOR? WHY DOES EVERYONE WHO JOINS NEVER COME BACK AND WHAT IS ON THE OTHER SIDE OF THE DOOR

WHERE DO THE RECRUITS GO AFTER SIGNING UP?

AN EXISTENTIAL LOVE STORY THAT ASKS QUESTIONS OF WHO WE ARE, WHAT WE WANT FROM LIFE AND WHETHER WE'RE GETTING IT, THE RECRUITMENT OFFICER IS A REMODELLING OF THE 1706 PLAY BY GEORGE FARQUHAR. *THE RECRUITING OFFICER*

Writer's Block

By

Thomas Alexander

Paul Block was once a prolific writer. A recipient of both the Pen and Faulkner awards and the author of over ten different novels, he was once considered the UK's most up and coming writer until, at the age of forty, he suffered a nervous breakdown.

Ten years later the world has forgotten Paul Block. Holed up in his study he has been working on the same first page of his new novel for nearly five years, kept company by only his maid, a foul mouthed Irish hit-man, a veteran of the battle of Gettysburg and a nineteen forties femme fetal.

Today, all that's going to change. Paul has a busy day ahead of him. First he's going to kill a persistent and charmless young reporter who wants to do a piece on 'writer's block' and then he's going to have a rare visit from his son who's bringing him bad news and a new couch.

With a missing body and a son who hates him, Paul must finally rid himself of his protagonists if he's ever going to stay out of jail, and finish that first page.

THOMAS

Japan, 1945 – A Family At War

When a wandering priest escaping a troubled past is taken in by a prominent family, a quiet city in northern Japan is forced to confront the dark shadows of war seeping into their lives in ways they could never have anticipated.

With its townsmen scattered throughout the farthest ends of a desperate empire in a final defence against the encroaching West, the idyllic northern city of Morioka, far removed from the harsh realities of the front, is largely left to itself.

THOMAS ALEXANDER

A Scattering of Orphans

But when a prominent doctor is conscripted and sent to Manila, his sister is left as head of the household and must deal with a young priest living at the bottom of their garden with a large collection of maps and strange knowledge of English.

As the cold hand of war approaches, each person must choose their own destiny and place in the new world.

THE OTHER SIDE

DIRECT LIGHT

Thomas Alexander

WRITING WILLIAM